TWO CANTATAS
FOR SOPRANO AND CHAMBER ENSEMBLE

Recent Researches in the Music of the Baroque Era is one of four quarterly series (Middle Ages and Early Renaissance; Renaissance; Baroque Era; Classical Era) which make public the early music that is being brought to light in the course of current musicological research.

Each volume is devoted to works by a single composer or in a single genre of composition, chosen because of their potential interest to scholars and performers, and prepared for publication according to the standards that govern the making of all reliable historical editions.

Subscribers to this series, as well as patrons of subscribing institutions, are invited to apply for information about the "Copyright-Sharing Policy" of A-R Editions, Inc., under which the contents of this volume may be reproduced free of charge for performance use.

Correspondence should be addressed:

A-R Editions, Inc.
315 West Gorham Street
Madison, Wisconsin 53703

RECENT RESEARCHES IN THE MUSIC OF THE BAROQUE ERA • VOLUME XXVII

Louis-Nicolas Clérambault

TWO CANTATAS FOR SOPRANO AND CHAMBER ENSEMBLE

Edited by Donald H. Foster

A-R EDITIONS, INC. • MADISON

Copyright © 1979, A-R Editions, Inc.

ISSN 0484-0828

ISBN 0-89579-104-8

Library of Congress Cataloging in Publication Data:

Clérambault, Louis Nicolas, 1676-1749.
   [L'Ile de Délos]
   Two cantatas.

   (Recent researches in the music of the baroque era ;
v. 27 ISSN 0484-0828)
   Words in French.
   CONTENTS: L'Ile de Délos.—La muse de l'opéra.
   1. Solo cantatas, Secular (High voice)—Scores.
I. Clérambault, Louis Nicolas, 1676-1749. La muse de
l'opéra. 1978. II. Series.
M2.R238   vol. 27   [M1613.3]   780'.903'2s   [782.8'2'54]
ISBN 0-89579-104-8   78-21855

Contents

Preface

The Composer and His Works

Louis-Nicolas Clérambault (1676-1749) was the son of a member of the Twenty-four Violins of the King and early showed an aptitude for music. His principal teachers were the organist André Raison (d. 1719), to whom he dedicated his only book of organ music, and the composer Jean-Baptiste Moreau (1656-1733). Clérambault's first known published composition dates from 1697; it was the first of eight songs published in volumes of the annual series *Airs sérieux et à boire* between 1697 and 1714. Also in this period were published the *Livre de pièces de clavecin* (1702),[1] the *Livre d'orgue* (around 1710), the first two of his five books of cantatas (I, 1710; II, 1713), and the first of his five separate cantatas, *Le Bouclier de Minerve* (1714).

Clérambault's justly famous cantata *Orphée*, from the first book of cantatas, brought him to the attention of Louis XIV. The stern Mme de Maintenon, the king's wife in later years, had been responsible for the decline of operatic productions at court since she favored private musical *soirées* in her apartments three or four times a week. It must have been at one of these concerts that *Orphée* was performed, with the flattering result that Louis XIV gave Clérambault some texts to set to music—those in the third book, by unknown authors—and named him superintendent of Mme de Maintenon's private concerts. We do not know if Clérambault actually served in this position, but in about 1715, apparently with Mme de Maintenon's help, he was appointed organist at her school for daughters of impoverished noblemen, the Maison Royale de Saint-Louis at Saint-Cyr, and at the church of Saint-Sulpice in Paris.[2] Both positions had formerly been held by Guillaume-Gabriel Nivers (ca. 1632-1714). In that same year (1715) Clérambault dedicated a new publication, his only sacred cantata, *Abraham*, to Mme de Maintenon, calling it "homage worthy of your kindnesses." The following year saw publication of the two cantatas in the present edition, *L'Ile de Délos*, one of the four works in the third book, and *La Muse de l'Opéra*, issued separately. In a preliminary notice in the third book, Clérambault says that the four works comprising it had been performed before Louis XIV, and this had "excited in the public a gratifying eagerness to have them." The first of the four works in Book III, *Apollon*, is subtitled in the table of contents "Cantate pour le Roy."

Sometime between 1716 and 1720 Clérambault assumed a third position, that of organist at the church of the Jacobins de la rue Saint-Jacques, a post formerly held by his teacher Raison. From then until his death

Clérambault divided his time among his three positions; he later had the assistance of his sons César-François-Nicolas and Evrard-Dominique. In 1720 Clérambault's fourth book of cantatas was published, containing just two works. This was followed in 1721 by *Le Soleil vainqueur des nuages*, a single cantata in celebration of the recovery of the young Louis XV from a serious illness. The fifth and final book of cantatas, again comprising only two works, appeared in 1726. Evidently Clérambault dedicated the fifth book to Marie Leszczinska, Louis XV's new bride, in an effort to win from her the same kind of favor that Mme de Maintenon had shown him. Clérambault had also become known for the private concerts—one of several such concert series in Paris at the time—given in his home on the Rue du Four.[3]

In 1733 he brought out two volumes of songs and motets, composed by himself and Nivers, for Saint-Cyr. Another volume of music for Saint-Cyr and similar institutions is undated, but must have been published about 1720 or after because Clérambault's position at the Jacobins is listed on the title page. In 1733, he also became associated with the series *Nouvelles Poésies spirituelles et morales sur les plus beaux airs de la musique françoise et italienne* (1730 to after 1733; 2nd ed. of Vols. I-IV, 1737-?), serving as editor of the figured bass in the fourth through the eighth volumes. Of twenty-four of Clérambault's own songs in the series,[4] thirteen are arias from his cantatas supplied with religious texts and sometimes with simplified music.

Clérambault's last cantata, *Les Francs-maçons*, bears witness to his membership in the Freemasons; he was one of many musicians then belonging to the order in France. His name appears in the books of one of the earliest French lodges, Coustos-Villeroy, from the time of its founding in 1736.[5] The order's religious outlook was highly suspect in France, and it was forced underground in 1737-8 by the persecutions of Cardinal Fleury. It is no accident that *Les Francs-maçons* was published in 1743, the year of Fleury's death.[6]

In 1745 Clérambault participated in the elaborate week-long dedicatory ceremonies for the new church of Saint-Sulpice, culminating in a final service that included "the motets of the Holy Sacrament, the Holy Virgin, the dedication of the church, and the prayer for the king, all composed by M. Clérambault and performed by nearly one hundred musicians, the elite of Paris and Versailles. . . ."[7] The same year Clérambault had two *idylles*—cantata-like works for soloists and chorus—performed by the girls of Saint-Cyr and then published; one composition honored the marriage of the dauphin and Maria Theresa, and the other celebrated Louis XV's departure for a military campaign.

Clérambault seems to have been active until his final year. In 1748 he composed a motet for the dedication of an altar[8] and a *divertissement*, now lost, for a comedy given at the Collège Louis-le-Grand. Clérambault was survived after his death in 1749 by a daughter and two sons. His sons continued in his steps, filling his positions and reissuing some of his cantatas. Among Clérambault's unpublished works are five volumes of motets, many songs and motets in the volumes of music for Saint-Cyr, and a few instrumental chamber works.[9]

The Music

The vogue for Italian music in France was in full swing in the first years of the eighteenth century;[10] regular performances of such music were causing the well-known controversies between traditionalists, such as Le Cerf de la Viéville, and modernists, such as Raguenet. The Lullists found Italian music bizarre, harmonically outrageous, and full of awkward leaps and other difficulties; the Italianists found traditional French music too simple, unchanging, and uninteresting. French solo chamber cantatas began as direct imitations of Italian models. Moved by the spirit of the *réunion des deux goûts*, nearly every popular composer of cantatas—Morin, Bernier, Batistin, Campra, Clérambault, Jacquet de la Guerre, Bourgeois, Courbois, Montéclair, and others—combined Italian and French traits in various ways. The craze for the cantata was short-lived, however; the popularity of the form, which began around 1705 and peaked in the second decade of the century, was already on the wane by the 1750s. After this, cantatas were largely replaced by smaller, more trivial works called *cantatilles*.[11]

During this period, Clérambault—though known as a good organist and composer of motets—was often cited as the best of the cantata composers. Perhaps J. Bachelier, in a Dutch collection of French cantata texts published in 1728, expressed this opinion in the most colorful manner of all:

> M. Clérambault's cantatas have received the admiration of all of Paris. When a Frenchman was attending our concerts [in Holland] and heard cantatas of Messrs. Batistin and Bernier performed, he said to us with surprise: "What, Messieurs, is Clérambault not known to you? What! You never sing his *Orphée*, his *Médée, Pygmalion, Léandre et Héro*, or his *Musette*? There you have pieces of the utmost beauty, and one finds few others comparable to them in grace of melody, forcefulness of accompaniment, and difficulty of execution." It was replied to him that these cantatas that he had just praised were known, and their merit fully recognized, and that for this reason they were not profaned so much as to be made use of every day; that they were reserved for the high holy days and for Sundays; and that to be all the more prepared, those of Messrs. Bernier and Batistin were used as lessons.[12]

Clérambault's cantatas were widely performed at the *Concerts spirituels*, Marie Leszczinska's *Concerts de la reine*, and even at the Opéra; all these performances are detailed in the *Mercure de France*. Some of the cantatas were reprinted so often that worn-out plates had to be replaced. The cantatas in Books I and II, especially *Orphée*, were by far the most known and praised, since Clérambault's later ones were issued largely after the genre's peak of popularity. *Orphée* and three other cantatas from Books I and II were parodied in an amusing manner by the author and composer, Nicolas Grandval.[13]

Clérambault's twenty-five cantatas are a veritable compendium of the genre, ranging from *galant* ones like *L'Amour piqué par une abeille* to the larger dramatic ones for which he was chiefly known—*Orphée, Médée, Léandre et Héro*, and *Pyrame et Thisbé*. In overall form, they range from the conventional three-recitative–three-aria design (R-A-R-A-R-A) to the unusual arrangements in *L'Ile de Délos* (Prélude-A-A-A-R-A-R-A-R-R-*mesuré*-A) and *La Muse de l'Opéra* (Prélude-R-A-Tempête-R-A-A-*Scène infernale*-R-A). The cantatas are scored for various vocal forces: fifteen are for soprano; two are for high tenor (*haute contre*); five are for bass; two are for two voices (soprano-*haute contre*, and soprano-bass); and one is for three voices (soprano-soprano-bass). Clérambault's Italianate compositional characteristics include a preference for driving rhythmic figures like ♪♫♫ , occasional *bizarreries* like wide leaps or unexpected harmonies, and frequent *da capo* arias that often include motto-like beginnings in which the voice sings part of the opening phrase, is interrupted by the accompanying instruments, and then combines with them for the entire phrase. Clérambault's French side appears in his several French-overture-like preludes, his delicately ornamented slow arias, his short and simple *airs gracieux*, and his recitative style, which frequently has the changing meters and melodic gestures of the Lully tradition. Some cantatas contain more Italian characteristics than others; this is especially true in regard to Book I. Clérambault's third book, on the other hand, is the most consistently French in style. Both styles are found, however, in all twenty-five works.

Clérambault's cantatas cover a wide range of subject types—*galant*, heroic, allegorical, pastoral, sacred, Anacreontic, and descriptive.[14] *L'Ile de Délos* and *La Muse de l'Opéra* are the only cantatas in the last category; there is no story, and these two texts (anonymous, like most of those Clérambault set) apparently served no further purpose than to give the composer an opportunity to employ imitative effects. The subject of *L'Ile de Délos* concerns Apollo and the Muses on the island of Delos, and the text refers to the sounds of bird songs, leaves rustling, echoes, and the playing of the musette, or bagpipes. *L'Ile de Délos* could be interpreted as a tribute to Louis XIV; however, it is more subtle than the other Apollo cantata in Book III, in which Louis is named in the text. In *La Muse de l'Opéra*, the narrator, presumably one of the Muses, describes several of the standard operatic situations—a battle, a hunt, a country scene with dancing, a storm, a woodland scene with birds, sleep, and infernal tumult. A concluding maxim points up the illusoriness of pleasure:

> Dans ce qui flatte vos désirs
> Croyez tout ce qu'on fait paraître;
> On voit s'envoler les plaisirs
> Lorsque l'on cherche à les connaître.

The subject matter of the cantata and the fact that copies of the work were sold at the Paris Opéra[15] suggest a possible connection with the Opera Balls—the *Bals de l'Opéra*—which began in January of the same year (1716) in which *La Muse de l'Opéra* was published. These gala events were held at various times and one could attend either masked or unmasked.[16] Machinery had been installed in the theater so that both the main floor and the stage could be transformed into one continuous floor, while the boxes were still available for spectators. The Opera Ball itself is depicted in at least one anonymous cantata text, which appeared in 1716 in the *Mercure de France*.[17]

Performance Practice

Instrumentation

Both *L'Ile de Délos* and *La Muse de l'Opéra* are somewhat unusual from the standpoint of instrumentation. The most common instrumentation in French cantatas of the early eighteenth century, including those by Clérambault, is one or more violins, sometimes with one or more flutes, and continuo; there are seldom more than two upper instrumental voices. In *L'Ile de Délos* this standard instrumentation is used, but the scoring is much more detailed and varied than usual.

In *La Muse de l'Opéra*, the instrumentation—in keeping with the subject of its text—brings to mind not the cantata, but the opera. The score calls for several additional instruments, resulting in an ensemble nearly as large as a chamber orchestra. The incompleteness of instructions given in its score presents some of the same problems encountered in French opera scores of the period—the makeup of the continuo group, the choice of stringed-bass instruments, the meaning of *tous* in various contexts, and the extent to which wind instruments should be used are not precisely known. The movements of *La Muse de l'Opéra* may be grouped by their instrumental scoring as follows:

Four movements (Nos. 1, 7, 8, and 10) with undesignated continuo instruments and with the single upper instrumental staff marked *tous* (Nos. 1 and 8) or *tous•violons* (Nos. 7 and 10, giving way once in No. 10 to *hautbois seul*).

One (No. 6) with two instrumental staves, *flûte allemande seule* and *violons* (and no continuo part).

One (No. 4) with one upper voice, unspecified, and two bass voices on separate staves, labeled *basses de violon* and *contrebasse et basse continue*.

One (No. 3) *da capo* aria with contrasting instrumentation in each of the two sections: (A) two upper staves, labeled *trompette et premier dessus de violon* and *deuxième dessus de violon*, and two lower staves, labeled *timbales et basses de violon* and *basses de viole et continues*; and (B) one upper staff, alternating between one unspecified voice and two voices marked *hautbois*, and the continuo staff, marked *bassons* in those places where the oboes play.

Three recitatives (Nos. 2, 5, and 9), in which the continuo instruments are not given.

Some of the questions raised by this scoring may be answered with greater certainty than others. For example, the unlabeled part in No. 4 is clearly for violins alone, both because of the violinistic style and because of the range, g-d''', which is too low for either flutes or oboes. In No. 8 the single word *tous* also seems to mean violins alone for the same reasons. In the "Prélude" (No. 1), however, neither style nor range would so limit the part marked *tous*; on the contrary, this part could be played on all of the high winds scored for in the cantata, and the nature of the movement suggests fuller instrumentation as well.

In the Lullian orchestra, flutes and oboes were always played by the same performers;[18] since parts for two oboes, for one oboe, and for one flute appear at different times in *La Muse de l'Opéra*, at least two woodwind players are necessary. The violins in the "Prélude" could easily be doubled by either two oboes or by one oboe and one flute. The former doubling is the more probable, and if it is done, one or two bassoons should be added to the continuo line, as was traditional in the Lullian orchestra.

The designation *tous•violons* is not as precise as it might seem. In No. 7 ("Sommeil") *tous•violons* probably means violins alone, though a flute could be added with good effect, because the movement is soft throughout. On the other hand, in No. 10, with its alternating dynamic levels, *tous•violons* seems to include oboes, for reasons to be explained below.

The oboe is actually specified in only two places in *La Muse de l'Opéra* (Nos. 3 and 10) and the bassoon in only one (No. 3). Apart from the section in No. 10 marked *hautbois seul*, this double-reed writing (for both oboes and bassoons) is all in the B-section of No. 3 (mm. 91-143). At the beginning of this section, no instrumentation is indicated, even though the total number of instrumental staves in the original publication drops from four to three and both text and music change in mood from martial to pastoral. Oboes and bassoons are not mentioned until mm. 99-100. They are specified again in two other spots (mm. 122-3 and 137-8) that are similar to mm. 99-100. This scoring corresponds almost exactly to Lully's soloistic use of double reeds in pastoral scenes, where *ritournelles* are scored for two oboe parts and one bassoon part, probably doubled by low strings. Because such woodwind trios (two oboes and one bassoon) were considered to be more penetrating than violins, they sometimes served as short, loud interludes between softer string-accompanied sections, providing a contrast in dynamics as well as in timbre.[19] This seems to be the case in No. 3, since the double reeds are indicated only when the voice rests. The whole B-section, therefore, should probably be performed by violins *alternating* with oboes, and by viols *joined* three times (mm. 90-1, 113-14, and 128-9) by bassoons, plus the harpsichord. On the other hand, if the double-reed instruments played only where marked, they would have very little to do; the bassoons, for example, would play a total of nine notes on three pitches, E, A, and d. The double reeds probably were also expected to play in the A-section, although they are not mentioned there. Perhaps the solution to the problem of incomplete instructions as to when the double reeds should play lies in the detailed dynamic markings—*doux* and *fort*—throughout the A-section. Such markings "in Lully's day . . . could refer not only to the degree of volume of a single instrument, but also to the strength of instrumentation."[20] Since the double reeds were loud instruments and sometimes doubled the strings in three-voiced writing, and since they are scored for later in this aria, *doux* may have been meant to show the double reeds where to rest and *fort* may have indicated where to bring them back in. It is not surprising that this practice of cueing the double reeds is not completely consistent, considering the casual attitude toward such things at the time. A few editorial additions have been made here for the sake of consistency. Furthermore, the dynamic markings in the highest staff do not refer to the presence or absence of the trumpet, because it is designated separately (*doux et sans trompette*). One might well ask why its directions are so specific if the double reeds were meant to play through this section with no mention whatsoever. The answer is that in the opera-orchestra tradition of the early eighteenth century, double reeds were commonly not named in the score, but orchestra parts show that they did indeed play much of the time.[21] There was no reason to specify this standard *col parte* technique in the A-section; only in the B-section, where oboes play *alone*, was it necessary to name them. The same principles have been applied in editorial suggestions for instrumentation in No. 10, with two exceptions: (1) Once (mm. 58-9) "*fort*" at the beginning of a phrase is followed only one measure later, where the voice enters, by "*doux*." Because this is the final phrase of the aria, an exception is apparently made by scoring for voice and double reeds together; "*fort*" cues the double reeds in, and "*doux*" warns them to play softly. (2) In the special circumstance where the solo oboe is used in a duet with the voice

(mm. 101 ff.), the added weight of bassoons in the bass is probably unnecessary.

Of the two sizes of trumpet used in France in the period, C and D, the former would have been used for the trumpet part of No. 3 (A-section); the part fits the C-trumpet perfectly, using only the natural notes g', c", d", e", f", g", a". These tones are almost the only ones found in Lully's trumpet writing, in contrast to the higher notes common in other countries.[22] The trumpet is accompanied in No. 3 by timpani, as it generally is in baroque scores—indeed, for Lully, the two instruments were virtually inseparable. Two pairings of timpani were in common use in France, c G and d A.[23]

Three different low-stringed instruments are scored for in *La Muse de l'Opéra*. The *basse de viole*, or bass viol (tuned A_1, D, G, c, e, a, d'),[24] was the usual stringed-bass instrument for French continuo parts during Clérambault's period, not only in cantatas, but also in instrumental chamber music, where from the time of Lully it had served as the bass to two violins.[25] The *basse de viole* had a tone which was softer and more flexible than that of the larger *basse de violon*, and it was capable of playing much higher with greater ease because of its *chanterelle*—the topmost string.

The *basse de violon*, according to Michel Corrette's violoncello method *Méthode théorique et pratique* (1741), was the French stringed-bass instrument "des anciens." It was tuned B_1-flat, F, c, g and was both larger and more difficult to play than the Italian cello, which Corrette says had replaced the *basse de violon* in France "for about twenty-five or thirty years," or in about 1710-15.[26] However, the term *basse de violon* apparently continued to be used in France for both the newer and the older instruments, and it is difficult to say which of the two instruments was intended in scores dating from around 1710 and after. *La Muse de l'Opéra* (1716) is from just this period, and calls for *basses de violon* in two of its movements, Nos. 3 and 4. The range of the part, C_1 to e'-flat, strongly suggests the cello, on which it would have to be played today in any case. The writing in the part is curiously dissimilar in each of the two movements: in No. 3 the part simply doubles the timpani; in No. 4, the "Tempête," the writing is as florid and virtuosic as that of the accompanying violins. In only one respect are the two movements alike for the *basses de violon*—in neither do they play the continuo line.

The *contrebasse* was apparently a version of the modern double bass, called in Brossard's *Dictionnaire de musique* the *violone* or *double basse*, "whose body and neck are about twice as big as those of the ordinary *basse de violon*, . . . and consequently the sound is an octave lower. . . ."[27] This was the period when the instrument was first becoming known in France as the bass in large choral works (Brossard tells us), as well as in the opera orchestra, where it was introduced by Montéclair and Sagioni. Corrette, in his method for the instrument, states that in the opera the *contrebasse* was used "only in storms, subterranean noises, and invocations, and kept a rather inopportune silence in the rest."[28] This is exactly the use of the *contrebasse* in *La Muse de l'Opéra*—it plays only in the "Tempête," (No. 4), where it provides the standard rumbling, and should not be used elsewhere in the cantata. One other "Tempête" appears in a cantata by Clérambault, *Léandre et Héro*, Book II (1713). It, too, has a part written for *contrebasse et clavecin*, with another for *basse de viole* and a third for *violons*. The *contrebasse* part there is similar to that in *La Muse de l'Opéra*. The *contrebasse* apparently sounded an octave lower than notated, because in both of these movements its part is often in unison with the *basse de violon* or *de viole* parts. Thus, the instrument for which the part was intended could go at least as low as B_3-flat—the lowest note in *Léandre et Héro*—whether by tuning or by *scordatura*. In *La Muse de l'Opéra* the *contrebasse* part goes to C_2, the lowest note of the modern double bass with extension.

The opera-like instrumentation in *La Muse de l'Opéra* raises a question about the harmony continuo instruments. The small select group, the *petit choeur*, within the French opera orchestra of the early eighteenth century, contained two theorboes—large lutes with several low drone strings—in addition to a harpsichord; all three instruments were used in the realization of continuo harmonies.[29] Although neither *La Muse de l'Opéra* nor any other cantata by Clérambault includes any mention of the theorbo, one might be added with good effect in No. 3, as well as elsewhere in the work. The beginning of No. 3 reads "basses de violes et *continues*" in the source, and this is the only such plural in Clérambault's cantatas; when the word *continue* appears again in the source, at the beginning of the following movement, its usual singular form is used. Besides referring to the harpsichord, *continues* could refer to the bassoons that probably played during No. 3; it does not indicate the *basses de violon*, because they have a separate part, nor does it refer to the *contrebasse*, because this instrument was not used in a movement of this sort.

For modern performances of either of these cantatas, compromises in instrumentation may have to be made; this is a notion that in itself is not entirely out of keeping with baroque practices. The instrumental demands of *L'Ile de Délos* are fairly modest; apart from the continuo, only violins and flutes are required. The use of the plural in the labeling of some of the parts for these instruments (*violons* and *flûtes allemandes*) clearly indicates that at least two of each instrument are needed, but because of the thinness of texture and the pastoral nature of the work, probably no more than this would be desirable. Although the continuo instruments are not designated (except in *bassetti*, where the violins take over this function—see below), they probably should be the bass viola da gamba and the harpsichord for the following reasons: (1) The

range (B_1-a') and frequent high tessitura in *L'Ile de Délos* suggest the viol rather than the cello. (2) Although no instrumentation is given in most of the continuo parts in Clérambault's cantatas, the words *viole* or *basse de viole* and *clavecin* do appear several times within movements; the first two terms are used where the viol diverges from the harpsichord, and the third term appears either in the same places or in the phrase *violon et clavecin* at the beginning of a *bassetto*. Clérambault's normal continuo instruments, then, in *L'Ile de Délos* and in nearly every other cantata, appear to have been the viol and the harpsichord. A cello could be substituted for the viol, however, and when the part goes below the cello's range, notes could be taken up an octave (indicated in this edition by small bracketed notes). This substitution was apparently already common by the mid-eighteenth century; Corrette says in his cello method, "Although most authors of sonatas and cantatas at the beginning of the century composed basses for viols, . . . that does not, however, prevent the violoncello from playing them with good result, which serves not a little to diminish the success of the viol. . . ."[30]

La Muse de l'Opéra makes considerably greater instrumental demands: ideally, there should probably be four to six violins (two or three to a part *divisi* in No. 3), two oboes and one flute (one oboist might also play the flute), one trumpet, two viols (one for recitatives and a second to join in on arias), two cellos, two bassoons, one double bass, two timpani, and a harpsichord, plus the conjectural theorbo discussed above. In addition to eliminating the theorbo, a further practical step might be to reduce the number of stringed instruments to two violins, one viol, one cello, and one double bass, and to reduce the number of bassoons to one. Again, as in *L'Ile de Délos*, a cello could be substituted for the viol. In *La Muse de l'Opéra*, where separate parts for both of these instruments are written, the cello could play the viol's part in No. 3, leaving the timpanist to play alone, and then play the *basse de violon* part in No. 4 as written, leaving the double bass to play with the harpsichord.

English equivalents of the names of instruments appearing in the present edition are as follows:

basse de viole = bass viola da gamba
basse de violon = cello
basson = bassoon
clavecin = harpsichord
contrebasse = double bass
dessus de hautbois = oboe
dessus de violon = violin
flûte allemande = flute
hautbois = oboe
timbales = timpani
trompette = trumpet
viole = viola da gamba
violon = violin

Figured Bass

Figured-bass playing at the keyboard was an ever-changing art, varying from country to country, from player to player, and from performance to performance. Thus, any written-out realization is at best an abstraction. Those used to playing from the figured-bass line alone will wish to disregard the realizations in this edition altogether. For others, however, a few of the more important guidelines used in making the realizations are as follows: (1) since the realizations are intended only for the harpsichord, tied notes have been little used; (2) the style has been kept as simple and unmannered as possible in order to prevent the accompaniment from calling attention to itself; (3) the usual number of voices in the keyboard part is four, one in the left hand and three in the right; (4) common tones have usually been kept in the same voice; (5) the uppermost vocal or instrumental voice has not been doubled or exceeded for any length of time; (6) the character of the accompaniment has been varied slightly in accordance with the character of the movement; and (7) a few decisions have been made purely on the basis of what is hoped was *bon goût*.[31]

In two movements of *L'Ile de Délos*, Nos. 2 and 3, the long tied bass notes should be repeated by the harpsichordist to prevent them from dying away. On the other hand, in mm. 46-7, 60-2, 74-7, and 89-90 of No. 3 and throughout No. 4 of *La Muse de l'Opéra*, editorial footnotes suggest ways that the harpsichordist may omit some of the repeated bass notes, leaving the full rendition of these passages to the bowed continuo instruments. This was practiced by harpsichordists at the time,[32] and Clérambault himself also occasionally separates the keyboard and string parts, as in *L'Ile de Délos*, No. 1 (mm. 65-7), and *La Muse de l'Opéra*, No. 3 (mm. 114 ff.). The harpsichordist may also wish to leave the performance of some ornaments to the string player (especially in *L'Ile de Délos*, No. 1).

Two important aspects of continuo playing that are not indicated in the present edition are registration and arpeggiation; both can vary widely with individual taste and the performance situation. Eighteenth-century writers insist that the accompaniment must never cover the solo voices or instruments. Thus, the volume of the accompaniment must be varied when necessary, either by adding or omitting voices, by altering the style of playing, or by changing the registration. Changing registration is perhaps of greatest importance to one playing from a realized part, since it can be done without changing the notes. On most harpsichords, this will mean playing on one or two 8' stops most of the time, adding the 4' stop only with caution.

Arpeggiation is often referred to in treatises as a most important feature of French continuo style on the harpsichord: a persistence of the lute-playing tradition, it was used in recitatives, in slow, expressive arias, and on long notes. Arpeggiation was always sub-ject to the dictates of taste and prominently excluded from ensembles and fast arias.[33] The variety of theorists' statements on arpeggiation indicates that the practice must have taken many forms. Delair gives six different ways of arpeggiating a four-note chord, five ascending and one descending.[34] Rameau states that chords should be quickly rolled from the bottom with the lowest finger of the right hand playing at the same time as the bass.[35] Saint-Lambert strikingly describes subtleties of arpeggiation that could sometimes be brought into play, but only in recitatives:

> When one accompanies a long recitative, it is beautiful sometimes to remain for a long time on a chord, if the bass permits it, and to play the chords only at long intervals, providing that the bass has only long notes. Other times, after having struck a full chord which is being held for a long time, here and there a single note is restruck, but with such discretion that it seems that the harpsichord yields them up all by itself, without the consent of the accompanist.
>
> Other times, doubling the chord tones, all the notes are struck one after another in continual repetition, causing the harpsichord to make a crackling almost like musket fire (tremolo), but after having made this agreeable uproar for three or four measures, one stops suddenly on some great harmonic (consonant) chord, as if to rest there from the trouble that one has been put to in making all that noise.[36]

However, it is quite clear from written-out continuo parts, such as the many by Corrette,[37] that the normal accompaniments to arias were as simple and unobtrusive as possible. When chord arpeggiation is used, it should be appropriate and should in no way impair rhythmic clarity.

Four *bassetti* occur in *L'Ile de Délos*: No. 5, mm. 84-90; No. 9, mm. 6-30; and No. 10, mm. 26-31 and mm. 51-6. In a continuo part the term *bassetto* applies to any passage in a C or G clef, the appearance of which signified that the harpsichordist should play the full harmonies much higher on the keyboard than usual.[38] In all of the *bassetti* in Clérambault's cantatas, the violin is used as the bowed instrument of the continuo rather than the viol.

In addition to some of the standard French sources of the period, the editor has used an unpublished figured-bass treatise by Clérambault, "Règles de l'accompagnement,"[39] to interpret the bass figures. "Règles de l'accompagnement" is a small autograph manuscript, signed and dated 1716. After discussing some basic elements of music, Clérambault gives the notes that must accompany various intervals above each ascending and descending scale degree in order to produce the desired harmonies. Unfortunately, the examples in Clérambault's treatise consist only of a bass line and figures. As in other treatises of the time, the seventh is automatically added in certain situations, such as the harmonization of scale-degrees 2 and descending 6 by the *petite sixte* $\binom{6}{4}$, of ascending 4 and 7 by the *grande sixte* ($\overset{6}{\underset{3}{5}}$) and of the seventh over a tonic pedal by the *accord sensible* ($\overset{x7}{\underset{4}{5}}$ or, in minor, often $\overset{x7}{\underset{\underset{2}{4}}{\flat6}}$). Moreover, the seventh is always present in the second chord of a final 4-3 cadence.[40] These rules have guided the harmonizations in this edition, even though Clérambault's figures may be incomplete (6 for $\underset{3}{4}^{6}$, 4-3 for $\underset{4\text{-}3}{7}$, etc.). This incompleteness is perfectly in keeping with the abbreviated symbols commonly in use at the time.[41] Clérambault's rules for harmonizing ninths (that they should be accompanied by the seventh and third on scale-degrees 2 and 6; by the seventh, fifth, and third on 3, 4, and 5; and by the third and fifth on the tonic) have been applied much less rigorously, allowing the musical situation and the hand position to be the chief guides. Finally, the symbols ♂, #6, and x6 all signify a major sixth in the source, ⑤ indicates a diminished fifth, and x5 indicates a chromatically raised fifth.[42]

Of the published treatises, Campion's *Traité d'accompagnement et de composition* is of direct importance, not only because it, too, appeared in 1716, but also because Clérambault's approval of the treatise is reported by its author. The work is based on the Rule of the Octave, a standard formula for harmonizing the ascending and descending major and minor scales in all keys, which Campion claims to be the first to have published:

> M. Clérambault acknowledges that he grasped the meaning of this Rule the instant it was shown to him. I have similarly taught it at first glance to several teachers from among my friends, who have abandoned their former principles in order to use only these.[43]

The uses of the *petite sixte* and the *grande sixte* in the Rule of the Octave are the same as those outlined above. Clérambault's use of the diminished seventh chord is referred to in another figured-bass treatise, Corrette's *Maître de clavecin*: "See the lovely cantatas of M. Clérambault. These dissonances were apparently not to the taste of M. Lully, because none may be found in his operas."[44]

While there is nothing unusual about partly unfigured basses in music of this period, Clérambault's cantatas are nearly always consistently figured. In the B-section of No. 3 in *La Muse de l'Opéra* there are three unfigured pedal points with changing harmonies above them. This might appear to be a way of indicating *tasto solo*, especially when similar passages in other works (like *L'Ile de Délos*, No. 3) *are* figured. In this instance, however, a clue comes from the arrangement of the aria in *Nouvelles Poésies*, Vol. IV, where two of these three unfigured pedal-point passages do contain the expected x7 for the *accords sensibles*. Full harmonizations for the harpsichord have therefore been pro-

vided in all three of the passages of *La Muse de l'Opéra*, No. 3, in the present edition.

Rhythm

Both *L'Ile de Délos* and *La Muse de l'Opéra* present some of the uncertainties of rhythmic interpretation—the problems of inequality and the relationship of duple and triple rhythms—that are characteristic of French baroque music. Editorial suggestions concerning rhythmic interpretation appear in the score; the comments below provide fuller explanations of these suggestions.

Inequality of certain note values in certain kinds of music was taken for granted by French musicians.[45] In keeping with this practice, inequality of the appropriate note values has been suggested in footnotes to the music pages of *L'Ile de Délos*, Nos. 2, 3, 4, and 5, and *La Muse de l'Opéra*, Nos. 1 and 7. Inequality was applied only to pairs of notes which were usually, if not exclusively, interpreted as long-short, so the formulae

$$\musSixteenthPair = \musDottedEighthSixteenth^3 \quad (\musRestSixteenth = \musRestDottedEighth^3) \text{ and } \musEighthPair = \musDottedQuarterEighth^3 \quad (\musRestEighth = \musRestDottedQuarter^3)$$

or

$$\musDottedEighthSixteenth = \musQuarterEighthTriplet^3 \text{ and } \musDottedQuarterEighth = \musHalfQuarterTriplet^3$$

have been used in these footnotes as approximations. The actual degree of alteration could vary from one movement to another and was a matter of personal preference, so that, for example, $\musSixteenthPair$ might be nearer to $\musUnequalPair^5$ in one movement, to $\musDottedEighthSixteenth^3$ in another, and to $\musDottedEighthSixteenth$ in another. Inasmuch as inequality was always subject to taste, the completely even performance of some of these movements is also a possibility if it is felt that the music is best served by it.

In the four movements discussed below, the question of unequal performance is further complicated by the editor's having to choose between separating or assimilating duple and triple rhythms.

L'Ile de Délos, No. 1—The chief difficulty here is that the rhythmic patterns $\musTripletEighths$, $\musTripletSixteenths$, $\musDottedEighthSixteenth$, and $\musEighthPair$ are all encountered, although the primary motion is in triplets. The careless vertical alignment of notes in the original edition offers no help at all. However, it is significant that two voices share the same notehead in m. 45: $\musFigureA$ (resolved in this edition as $\musFigureB$) and in m. 67: $\musFigureC$. This shows that both $\musDottedEighthSixteenth$ and $\musEighthPair$ should be given triplet interpretation ($\musDottedEighthSixteenth^3$) in this movement, a practice by no means uncommon at the time.[46] On the other hand, when figures like $\musDottedEighthSixteenth$ and $\musTripletSixteenths$ appear consistently throughout a passage (as they do in mm. 10-14, 27-31, and in the highest instrumental part in mm. 42-4, 48-50, and 84-6), this editor feels that they should be unaltered. These passages are all in the nature of bird-song imitations, and to force them into triplet rhythms would rob them of their distinctiveness. They are *concertino* passages almost like the bird imitations in Vivaldi's *Summer Concerto*, and they need to stand apart from the prevailing movement of the *ripieno*. The vocal part should conform to triplet inequality throughout; it contains no difficulties except for m. 55, which could either be left as it is or adapted to triplet rhythm.

L'Ile de Délos, No. 10—Here inequality is established by the presence of a recurring figure marked to be played *evenly*. This figure is the Italianate ♫♩ which Clérambault specifies as even in other arias; he evidently wished to dissociate this figure from the French inequality surrounding it. In addition to the direction *croches égales* at the figure's first appearance, there is a dot above or below each of the four eighth-notes whenever they occur (except for three times, at mm. 46, 49, and 66, where the dots were obviously forgotten). Further notational features exist in this movement in the form of triplets toward the end of the aria, and the occasional appearance of ♫ immediately following the even figure. The inequality of eighth-notes should therefore probably be ♪. to conform to the triplets. Moreover, the figure ♫ should also be rendered as ♪., because by this notation Clérambault appears only to be reminding the performers to return to unequal eighths following the even figure. This practice is particularly understandable in places like mm. 10 and 12, which are melodically identical to the four eighth-notes of the even figure. Without dotted notation, performers would have been inclined to play these eighth-notes evenly. This use of dotted notes also occurs in the next movement to be considered.

La Muse de l'Opéra, No. 3—Rhythmically, this is an especially perplexing movement. There are at least five factors to contend with: (1) in instrumental fanfare passages with figures like ♫, ♫♫, ♫♫♫, and ♫ (such as mm. 10-26 and 33-9), the presence of mixed values and repeated notes makes inequality out of the question and triplet alteration pointless; (2) in the instrumental horn-call passages with ♫, ♫♫, ♫♫, and ♫ occurring both simultaneously and side by side (such as mm. 46-7 and 60-2), triplet assimilation of all rhythms seems to be the best solution; (3) much of the instrumental writing is stepwise paired eighth-notes obviously intended to be uneven, and sometimes interspersed with triplets (mm. 98, 110, etc.); (4) within these uneven sections are passages that, because of wide leaps, must be *even* (mm. 114, 116-20, 129, and 134-6); (5) the voice part, independent of the instrumental writing except in mm. 69-74, is a logical candidate for unequal eighth-notes everywhere but in these five measures. Certain details about the notation of repeated notes in this movement give some clues about the application of inequality throughout the movement. The continuo part in mm. 46-7, consisting of a single reiterated pitch, is in the rhythm ♫ throughout, because even eighth-notes on one pitch would not have been performed unevenly. In m. 48, when the part becomes stepwise, the notation

changes to even eighth-notes, which in that case *would* have been performed unequally. In other words, the dotted notation which was simply meant to insure uneven eighths (♪.) on repeated notes was an unnecessary precaution in stepwise eighth-note writing. In a parallel passage, mm. 60-3, the measure following the repeated notes is also in dotted rhythm, because its first three notes are separated by wide intervals, something that might have prompted performers to play them evenly. (In the *Nouvelles Poésies* version of this aria, this measure is notated ♫♫♫.) In the next measure, however, even notation is once again returned to because the eighth-notes are stepwise. In one other passage, the timpani part in m. 73, the repeated notes are even eighths because it is part of a fanfare section; in m. 74, however, the repeated notes are in the rhythm dotted-eighth-and-sixteenth in order to conform to the triplet rhythm which begins in that measure. Only once, in m. 89, do the fanfare duplets and hunting-horn triplets occur simultaneously. Taken as a whole, *La Muse de l'Opéra,* No. 3 is a particularly varied movement in which the voice part, written almost entirely with uneven eighth-notes, is accompanied by several contrasting kinds of music, some with unaltered note values and some with triplet assimilation of all figures. This treatment is, of course, in keeping with the series of varied scenes that the text depicts. (The editorial suggestions concerning rhythm in mm. 98, 110, and 129 of the voice part are conjectural.)

La Muse de l'Opéra, No. 10—In this *da capo* aria, the rhythmic motion is primarily ♫ and ♫♫ up to the end of the instrumental ritornello before the B-section (m. 79), and ♫, ♫♫, and ♫♫♫ during the B-section. The direction *piqué* at the beginning of No. 10 refers to a strong degree of inequality in which "the first half-beat should have a dot."[47] In this aria *piqué* apparently refers to the performance of ♫ not assimilated into the triplet movement, but exactly as written (or *slightly* overdotted in the A-section), so that the sixteenth-note falls after the final note of the triplet in the A-section, but fits precisely into the duple rhythms of the B-section. (Again, the editorial suggestions in mm. 6, 17, 26, 42, 46, 64, and 72 are conjectural.)

The meter signatures of the two cantatas are all in modern use except 2 and 3, which appear in this edition as $\frac{2}{[2]}$ and $\frac{3}{[4]}$. Clérambault's recitatives, true to the Lullian tradition, make ample use of metrical change. Although some of the meters he uses elsewhere in recitatives present some problems of interpretation,[48] the ones in the cantatas of this edition are quite clear. In accordance with the practice of the early eighteenth century, a quarter-note in C or 3 is the approximate equivalent of a half-note in ₵, 2, or $\frac{3}{2}$, and this is indicated as either [♩=♩] or [♩=♩] in the score of the present edition. However, meters and note values were approximate in these recitatives, and the text should also help to determine rhythm and speed.[49]

Ornamentation

The mastery of the intricacies of ornamentation was one of the chief assets of the well-trained French singer or instrumentalist. At the distance of two hundred years, the modern performer has a difficult task in comprehending the art of ornamentation in all of its variety and inconsistency. Studies by modern authors, such as Aldrich and Neumann,[50] make the subject more approachable, and the performer will do well to become familiar with them. This editor gives only the briefest introduction to Clérambault's *agréments*, dealing specifically with those found in *L'Ile de Délos* and *La Muse de l'Opéra.*[51]

Clérambault's cantatas are heavily ornamented, especially in slow, expressive arias. Ornaments sometimes occur in quick succession and, in slow arias, in as many as three voices at once. All of this strongly suggests that additional ornaments in performance are neither necessary nor desirable. In contrast to the great variety of symbols in his keyboard music, Clérambault used only four ornament signs in the cantatas, namely, the cross, the small note, the long trill, and the turn.

The most common sign by far is the cross (+). Although it could indicate either an unspecified ornament or a trill, the cross in Clérambault's cantatas can usually be performed as a trill, and occasionally as a mordent. On shorter notes (such as the eighths and sixteenths in *L'Ile de Délos*, No. 9), the choices of interpretation of the + are limited to the short four-note trill ( ) or, especially when approached from a step below, the mordent ( ), which sometimes appears with *port de voix* ( ). On longer notes, however, the choice of ways' to perform the trill is wider: (1) the trill could begin where the main note begins or slightly before it; (2) the first note of the trill, the upper auxiliary, could be of any length, from as short as possible to almost the entire length of the main note, and could be either tied to or separated from the trill itself; (3) starting on the upper auxiliary (although the trill could also begin on the main note), the alternations of the trill notes could begin immediately and last through all or any portion of the main note, or, on a long trill in ensemble music, the main note could be held first and the trill begun half-way through; (4) the speed of the alternations could be fast, slow, or progressively accelerating; (5) a figure such as a turn or slide could be used to begin the trill; (6) the trill could be terminated by a sudden stop, a turn, or the anticipation of the next note. Clérambault frequently combines the cross with a written-out approach or termination (see *La Muse de l'Opéra*, No. 6). The cross appearing one or more times in the middle of a long tied note (as in *La Muse de l'Opéra*, No. 3, mm. 85-7) probably indicates one or more short trills in the course of the note's duration.

The *tremblement lié*[52] is a form of the trill that occurs very often in Clérambault's cantatas. In this figure, the trill is preceded by and tied to its upper neighbor. Therefore, a *tremblement lié* is any trilled note under a slur approached by step from above. The two main possibilities of interpretation are that the trill *anticipates* the time of the main note (Ex. 1a) or that it begins *on* the time of the main note (Ex. 1b), in either case usually beginning on the *pitch* of the main note. On short notes it must become a five- or even a three-note trill (Ex. 2).

Ex. 1.

Ex. 2a. *L'Ile de Délos*, [No. 7], m. 19

Ex. 2b. *L'Ile de Délos*, [No. 1], m. 2

Three signs specifically denoting a long trill appear in Clérambault's cantatas: *t* ﹏﹏﹏ , ﹏﹏﹏ , and ﹏﹏﹏. Although they are seldom used, all three signs appear in the two cantatas of this edition (*L'Ile de Délos*, Nos. 1 and 9; *La Muse de l'Opéra*, No. 10). The slight differences between the three signs are apparently of no significance; they all seem to indicate a continuous trill, and are used instead of the cross to insure this interpretation. The termination of the trill is usually written out, either as an anticipation (which should be preceded by a brief stop on the main note; see Ex. 3) or as a turn.

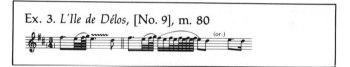

Ex. 3. *L'Ile de Délos*, [No. 9], m. 80

The appoggiatura, written as a single small note, is also an important ornament in Clérambault's cantatas. In these two works appoggiaturas are all at the interval of a second; however, appoggiaturas do occur, albeit infrequently, at the fourth and fifth elsewhere in Clérambault's music. The appoggiatura from a step below, the *port de voix*, was sometimes automatically embellished by a mordent so that = or or , etc. Only rarely is the *mordent* actually notated in Clérambault's cantatas, where it appears as , but the option of adding the mordent should certainly remain open to the performer. Considerable variety exists in the choice of rhythmic interpretation, ranging from taking the appoggiatura from the time of the preceding note to giving it half or even more than half of the time of the main note. The question of rhythmic interpretation is a controversial one,[53] but what is certain is that there is no one rigid interpretation that fits all cases. Each performer must decide whether to begin the appoggiatura on or before the beat and how long to make it on the basis of how well it fits with the other parts and with the harmony, and how musically suitable it is to his own part. (Ex. 4 shows some possibilities of interpretation.) Furthermore, when an appoggiatura is part of a recurrent figure in a movement, its performance should be consistent. Above all, the appoggiatura must not be allowed to alter the harmony, which, in Jean Rousseau's words, "is preferable to all melody" in these matters.[54]

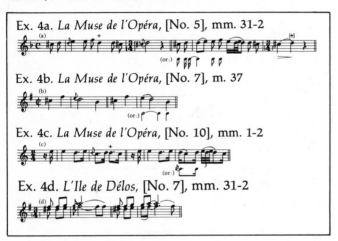

Ex. 4a. *La Muse de l'Opéra*, [No. 5], mm. 31-2

Ex. 4b. *La Muse de l'Opéra*, [No. 7], m. 37

Ex. 4c. *La Muse de l'Opéra*, [No. 10], mm. 1-2

Ex. 4d. *L'Ile de Délos*, [No. 7], mm. 31-2

One form of the appoggiatura that is exceptionally important in Clérambault's cantatas is the *tierce coulée* or passing appoggiatura. The *tierce coulée* is distinguishable from other forms only in context—it is always a passing tone between the two notes of a falling third, and is slurred to the second note. Although the *tierce coulée* is taken in the same articulation as the second note (and, in vocal music, shares its syllable), it is performed in time taken from the *previous* note. One proof of its existence in Clérambault's music appears in mm. 3 and 16 in the final aria of *La Muse de l'Opéra*, where the instrumental and vocal versions of the same phrase are notated differently, one having the ornament written out, and the other using the *coulé*. The *tierce coulée* should be employed frequently in Clérambault's cantatas, most often at the end of a phrase, where, indeed, no other interpretation of Clérambault's appoggiatura sign would be satisfactory (Ex. 5). Not every descending third with an appoggiatura is necessarily a *coulé*, however; sometimes the on-the-beat interpretation also seems suitable (*L'Ile de Délos*, No. 10, m. 24).

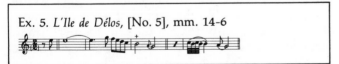

Ex. 5. *L'Ile de Délos*, [No. 5], mm. 14-6

Four other ornaments appear in the works of this edition: the slide (*L'Ile de Délos*, No. 3, m. 11; *La Muse de l'Opéra*, No. 6, m. 72); the turn (*La Muse de l'Opéra*, No. 6, mm. 38 and 43); the anticipation (*L'Ile de Délos*, No. 5, m. 46, and No. 7, m. 47); and the springer (*L'Ile de Délos*, No. 7, m. 26). All are infrequent in

Clérambault's cantatas and are written in either small or large notes, with the turn also indicated by the symbol ↝ .

Special care must be taken by the performers of these works when two or three ornaments occur simultaneously. Occasionally these simultaneous ornaments either differ from one another or are the same but occur on notes of different length (*La Muse de l'Opéra*, No. 6, mm. 69-74; *L'Ile de Délos*, No. 7, mm. 69 and 75). In such cases, the ornaments must be executed so that the harmony is clear and the voices fit together gracefully. In the majority of simultaneous ornaments, however, the same ornament occurs in all (usually two) voices on notes of the same length, and the problem then is one of synchronization. Trills, appoggiaturas, and—in other cantatas—slides are treated this way and need to be performed exactly together. In the case of long trills in thirds or sixths, such as those in *L'Ile de Délos*, No. 9, the performers must decide beforehand whether to begin the trills slowly and accelerate or to keep them at a steady speed, and whether to come to a stop on the main note before a termination or to go directly into the termination without pause. Twice in the last aria of *La Muse de l'Opéra* (mm. 104-7 and 116-19) the cross and long trill are used on long held notes in two voices at once. These measures are only a quarter of an inch long in the original edition, with the note heads in the middle of each measure and the crosses placed slightly after them. Thus, determining exactly where the ornaments should be placed is difficult, but they appear to occur after, rather than on, the first beat in each case. A possible solution for ornamentation problems in these measures is suggested editorially in a footnote on the appropriate page in the score.

Tempo and Expression Markings

L'Ile de Délos and *La Muse de l'Opéra* are liberally provided with indications of speed, mood, and volume. Those markings referring to tempo or to both tempo and mood include *fort gravement, lentement, sans lenteur, légèrement, gai, animé,* and *très vite.* Markings referring only to mood or style include *gracieusement, marqué, coulé* (flowing), *doucement* (gently), and *tendrement.*

In addition to Clérambault's usual directions for "soft" and "loud," *doux* and *fort* (not to be confused with the *fort* meaning "very" in directions like *fort tendrement*), *plus doux* and *plus fort* for "softer" and "louder" also appear. There are two echo sections, where loud and soft dynamics alternate. In one echo section, Clérambault appropriately uses the word *écho* in place of *doux* (*L'Ile de Délos*, No. 9, mm. 56 ff.), and in the other the echo effect is accomplished by changes in instrumentation as well as in dynamics—*fort, tous* alternates with *doux, sans trompettes* (*La Muse de l'Opéra*, No. 3, mm. 60 ff.) in the source.

Editorial Practice

In titles, texts, and directions in the score, the spelling, accents, punctuation, and capitalization have been modernized. The placement of sharps, flats, and naturals has been changed to conform to modern practice. Accidentals obviously meant to carry across the measure bar in the source appear in brackets in this edition. When an accidental is repeated in the source before every occurrence of a note in a measure, all but the first accidental are omitted. When the musical context only implies a cancellation of an accidental found earlier in a measure in the source, a natural sign appears within brackets in the edition. The natural, employed inconsistently and infrequently by Clérambault, is used on the staff according to present practice to replace the sharps and flats by which he usually altered notes affected by a key signature.

Figured-bass symbols appear in the source most often above the staff, less so below it, and occasionally, where the symbol consists of more than one figure, partly above and partly below the staff. Bass figures are also occasionally reversed or otherwise rearranged (e.g., $\frac{4}{6}$, $\frac{5}{6}$, $\frac{3}{6}$). In the present edition all figures are below the staff ^{4} and in their usual order. Figures have been editorially supplied only in cases of obvious omissions or mistakes.

Since in Clérambault's music the original placement of the cross—over, under, or before a note; and above, below, or on the staff—appears to have no bearing whatsoever on its interpretation, the cross is given here above both note and staff (except where two parts share the same staff). Inasmuch as this symbol usually signifies a trill, the editorial accidental added in brackets before some crosses ([#]+) indicates the chromatic alteration of the upper auxiliary suggested by the musical context.

Editorial slurs have been added only to indicate the number of notes to be sung to a single syllable when this is not already indicated in the source, and, occasionally, to make the slurring of a passage consistent. In no way are slurs intended to affect the equality or inequality of a passage. All added slurs are bracketed, thus [⌢].

Note values are unchanged except for obvious mistakes and inexact dotted rhythms, such as ♪ ♫ ; such corrections are explained in the Critical Notes. The common combination of ♫♪ and ♪♩ is always unaltered.

The same staff in the source is often shared by more than one part, such as by violin and voice alternately. Separate staves have been provided in most of these places without comment; where the situation calls for an explanation, it is given in the Critical Notes.

The indentations of the beginnings of movements are editorial. If the clef used in the source differs from that of the present edition, the original clef is shown in incipits given at the beginnings of indented movements. All other editorial additions are bracketed and/or explained in the Critical Notes.

Critical Notes

Abbreviations are as follows: vn. = violin; fl. = flute; Bc. = Basse continue; v. = voice. Pitches are given according to the system in which middle c is c', two-line c is c'', and so forth.

L'Ile de Délos

[No. 1]—Mm. 2-4, 8-10, 65-6, Bc. written in alto clef. M. 45, vns. and fls., rhythm is ♫♪.♫♪.♪♩. M. 52, vns. and fls., rhythm: ♪ ♪ ♪ .

[No. 3]—Mm. 1-16 and 17-32, Bc., S-curved lines replace separate ties thus:

[No. 4]—Mm. 1-4, Bc., see entry for [No. 3], mm. 1-16.

[No. 5]—M. 23, vn., note 1 is missing. At this point in the source, both violin and voice share the same staff, the last note of the violin part in m. 22 coming at the end of a brace, and the entrance of the voice coming at the beginning of the next one. The voice's entrance, the final half-beat of m. 22, is inserted at the beginning of this brace, but the last note of the violin's phrase is omitted, since it is obviously c''. Mm. 84-90, vns. and Bc., these mm. contain a *bassetto*: the violin part is not given a separate staff here in the source, but the continuo staff, in the French violin clef, is marked *violons et clavecin*; the return to the viol in m. 90 is marked by the word *basse* and a return to the bass clef in the source.

[No. 7]—Mm. 82-6, Bc., alto clef in the source.

[No. 9]—M. 6, third beat, through m. 38, vns. and Bc., these measures contain a *bassetto*; the continuo part is in the French violin clef, marked *violons et clavecin*. Both instruments share the same staff through m. 38. Mm. 28 and 29, fl. I and II or vn., long trill symbol extends to just above second note of tie in the source. Mm. 30-8, Bc., no rests are provided for the harpsichord in the source, but the absence of figures and the style of writing make it obvious that it should remain silent. Mm. 30-4 and 37-8, fl. I and II or vn., long trill symbol extends to approximately above the dot of prolongation, which does not follow the note immediately in the source but is placed on the beat to which the note is lengthened. M. 34, fl. and vn., rhythm is ♪ ♫ ♩ ♪ in the source. Mm. 40-82, all parts distributed on two staves as follows: voice (treble clef) and continuo (bass clef) alternating with *flûte allemande* (French violin clef) and *violon seul* (soprano clef). M. 55, see entry for mm. 30-4 and 37-8. M. 68, see entry for mm. 28 and 29. Mm. 80-1, see entry for mm. 30-4 and 37-8.

[No. 10]—M. 6, second beat, through m. 10, and mm. 18-20, 35-7, and 45, Bc., alto clef in the source. M. 11, vn. beat 1 is eighth, eighth, eighth in the source. Mm. 26-31 and 51-6, vns. and Bc., these measures contain *bassetti*: the violin part is figured and marked *violons et clavecin*, while the normal continuo staff contains rests; the two parts overlap in mm. 26, 31, and 56. M. 56, Bc., figured bass, sharp 2 is under note 2, followed by a horizontal line extending to just past note 4 in the source.

La Muse de l'Opéra

[No. 4]—The rhythms originally written

have been changed to

throughout the movement. Mm. 6 and 7, vn., third beat of each measure, rhythm, dotted eighth and 7 thirty-second-notes in the source.

[No. 10]—Mm. 107 and 119, v., beat 2 of each measure, rhythm is sixteenth, thirty-second, thirty-second, in the source.

Acknowledgments

This edition of the two cantatas has been made from copies in the University of Michigan Library. The editor is indebted to its staff for permitting the microfilming of the original publications and the reproduction of two pages from them in the present edition.

Donald H. Foster
College-Conservatory of Music
University of Cincinnati

August 1978

Notes

1. Shown by Geneviève Thibault, in "Notes sur une édition inconnue de Clérambault," *Revue de musicologie* LII (1966):210-11, to have been first published in 1702.

2. Her special interest in Saint-Sulpice is discussed in A. Geffroy, *Madame de Maintenon, d'après sa correspondance authentique . . .* (Paris: Hachette, 1887), II:350-1.

3. Joachim Christoph Nemeitz, *Séjour de Paris, c'est-à-dire, instructions fidèles, pour les voiageurs de condition*, French trans. of 2nd ed. (Leyden, 1727), pp. 69-70, footnote.

4. Not fourteen, as appears in Renée Girardon, "Clérambault," *MGG* (1952), II:1499.

5. Paris, Bibliothèque Nationale, Collection Joly de Fleury: "Avis et mémoires sur les affaires publiques," Registre No. 184, fols. 129-146: register of membership in the Coustos-Villeroy Masonic Lodge from December 18, 1736, to July 17, 1737.

6. For more on French Freemasonry in this period see Pierre Chevallier, *Les Ducs sous l'acacia* (Paris: Vrin, 1964).

7. *Cérémonies de la dédicace et consécration de l'Eglise de Saint-Sulpice* (Paris, 1745), p. 25.

8. From a poster, *Avis important aux paroissiens de Saint-Sulpice* (1748), Paris, Bibliothèque Nationale, Fol. Lk¹ 7178.

9. The present editor has discussed Clérambault's biography in greater detail in "Louis-Nicolas Clérambault and His *Cantates francaises*," 2 vols. (Ph.D. diss., University of Michigan, 1967, University Microfilms No. 68-7596), pp. 25-95, including such matters as the inconsistencies in addresses given in his published works, the identification of his signatures, and the confusion between Clérambault *père* and *fils* in some references of the period. Further information on the series *Nouvelles Poésies*, including identification of the thirteen arias, is found on pp. 98-100. The chief eighteenth-

century biographical sources are the *Mercure de France* (containing numerous references to the life and works, especially the death notice in the issue of January 1750, p. 200); Pierre-Louis d'Aquin de Château-Lyon, *Lettres sur les hommes célèbres dans la science, la littérature et les beaux-arts sous le règne de Louis XV* (Amsterdam, 1752), p. 90; Evrard Titon du Tillet [Evrard-Dominique's godfather], *Le Parnasse françois* (Paris, 1732), Supplement of 1743, "Moreau," pp. 663-4, and Supplement of 1755, "Clairambault [*sic*]," p. 57; and Jacques Lacombe, *Dictionnaire portatif des beaux-arts*, new ed. (Paris, 1759), p. 155. Important modern sources are André Pirro's Preface to Clérambault's *Livre d'orgue*, in *Archives des maîtres de l'orgue des XVIe, XVIIe, et XVIIIe siècles*, ed. Alexandre Guilmant and André Pirro (Paris: Durand, 1901), III:89-91; Lionel de La Laurencie, *L'Ecole française de violon de Lulli à Viotti* (Paris: Delegrave, 1922-4), I:143-51; and (see footnote 4) Renée Girardon's article "Clérambault" in *MGG*. Marie Bert, in "La Musique à la Maison Royale Saint-Louis de Saint-Cyr, son rôle, sa valeur," [Third] Part, *Recherches sur la musique française classique* V (1965):91-102, discusses motets for Saint-Cyr by Clérambault and Nivers, including two unpublished cantata-like works she believes to be by Clérambault *père*.

10. See Maurice Barthélemy, "Un Foyer musical en France au début du XVIIIe siècle: le Palais-Royal," *Cahiers musicaux* No. 14 (1957-8):27-35: Michel Le Moël, "Un Foyer d'italianisme à la fin du XVIIIe siècle: Nicolas Mathieu, curé de Saint-André-des-Arts," *Recherches sur la musique française classique* III (1963):43-8; and Paul-Marie Masson, "La Musique italienne en France pendant le premier tiers du XVIIIe siècle," *Mélanges Hauvette* (1934), pp. 353-65.

11. On the French cantata, see Eugen Schmitz, *Geschichte der weltlichen Solokantate*, 2nd ed. rev. (Leipzig: Breitkopf und Härtel, 1955), pp. 191-235; Denise Launay and Simone Wallon, "Kan-

tate—Die französische Kantate," *MGG* (1958), VII:575-81; Julien Tiersot, "Cantates françaises du XVIIIe siècle," *Le Ménestrel* LIV (1893):131-3, 140-2, 157-8, 164-5, 172-3, 180-1, and 188-9; Charles Malherbe, "Commentaire bibliographique," in Jean-Philippe Rameau, *Oeuvres complètes*, ed. Camille Saint-Saëns, Vol. III: *Cantates* (Paris: Durand, 1897), pp. ix-xxxi; and David Tunley, *The Eighteenth-Century French Cantata* (London: Dennis Dobson, 1974).

12. "Les Cantates de Mr. *Clérambault* ont fait l'admiration de tout Paris. Quand un François se trouvoit dans nos Concerts, & qu'il entendoit exécuter celles de Mrs. *Batistin & Bernier*, il nous disoit avec surprise, Eh! quoi, Messieurs, est-ce que *Clérambault* ne vous est pas connu? Quoi! vous ne chantez point son *Orphée*, sa *Médée*, son *Pigmalion*, *Léandre & Héro*, enfin sa *Musette*? Ce sont là des morceaux du dernier beau, & l'on en trouve peu qui leur soient comparables pour le gracieux du chant, la force de l'accompagnement, & la difficulté de l'exécution. On lui répondit, que l'on connoissoit ces Cantates, dont il venoit de faire l'Eloge, que l'on en faisoit tout le cas qu'elles méritoient, & que par cette raison on ne les prophanoit pas assez pour les mettre à tous les jours; qu'on les réservoit pour les bonnes Fêtes, & les Dimanches; & que pour s'y préparer d'autant mieux, on se servoit de celles de Mrs. *Bernier & Batistin*, comme de Leçons." J. Bachelier, ed., *Recueil de cantates, contenant toutes celles qui se chantent dans les concerts: pour l'usage des amateurs de la musique et de la poësie* (The Hague, 1728), Preface, pp. [xiii-xiv].

13. The present editor treats the material in this paragraph in detail in "Louis-Nicolas Clérambault and His *Cantates françaises*," Vol. I, Chap. III. The section of this chapter on Grandval's parodies also appeared in essentially the same form as "Parodies on Clérambault Cantatas by Nicolas Grandval," *Recherches sur la musique française classique* IV (1964):120-6.

14. These are seven of the eight varieties of *cantate française* subject discussed by Malherbe in Rameau, *Oeuvres complètes*, III:xiii. Only the comic type is not represented in Clérambault's works, the closest being *La Muse de l'Opéra*.

15. As may be seen from the title page: LA MUSE DE / L'OPERA / OU LES CARACTERES / LIRIQUES / CANTATE / *a voix seule et simphonie* / PAR MR CLERAMBAULT / *Se vend a Paris.* / *A la porte de l'Academie Royale de Musique:* / *Chez l'Auteur, rüe des canettes proche St Sulpice,* / *et chez le Sr Foucault, rüe St Honoré a la regle d'or.* / *Avec Privilège du Roy 1716.*

16. Described by Saint-Simon in *Memoirs of Saint-Simon on the Reign of Louis XIV and the Regency*, trans. Bayle St. John, 2nd ed. (New York: Willey Book Co., 1936), III: 323-4; the *bals* of a later period are described by Jacques-Bernard Durey de Noinville, *Histoire du théâtre de l'Opéra en France depuis l'établissement de l'Académie royale de musique, jusqu'à présent* (Paris, 1753), I:159-64.

17. *Mercure de France*, February 1716, pp. 70-6.

18. Jürgen Eppelsheim, *Das Orchester in den Werken Jean-Baptiste Lullys*, Münchner Veröffentlichungen zur Musikgeschichte, ed. Thrasybulos G. Georgiades, Vol. VII (Tutzing: Hans Schneider, 1961), p. 179. This valuable monograph on French orchestral practice in the late seventeenth and early eighteenth centuries is the chief source of information for this section on instruments. Although the book includes a glossary of terms at the back (with separate pagination), in which much of the material is summarized, there is no index.

19. Eppelsheim, *Das Orchester*, pp. 110-12, 197-200, 204, and 209.

20. Eppelsheim, *Das Orchester*, p. 222: ". . . Zu Lully's Zeit Angaben wie 'doux' (und entsprechend 'fort') sich nicht nur auf den Stärkegrad des einzelnen Instrumentes beziehen können, sondern auch auf die Stärke der Besetzung."

21. Eppelsheim, *Das Orchester*, pp. 197, 218, *et passim*.

22. Eppelsheim, *Das Orchester*, pp. 121-6.

23. Eppelsheim, *Das Orchester*, p. 132.

24. The seven-stringed viol was standard in late-seventeenth- and early-eighteenth-century France, and sources are unanimous in giving this tuning, the lowest string A_1. Jean Rousseau, in *Traité de la viole* . . . (Paris, 1687), p. 35, prefaces the tuning by saying, "Il n'y a qu'une manière d'accorder la Viole en France." Modern sources, such as Eppelsheim, *Das Orchester*, Anhang-Glossar, p. 38; Nicholas Bessaraboff, *Ancient European Musical Instruments* (New York: October House, 1941), p. 281; and Hans Bol, *La Basse de viole du temps de Marin Marais et d'Antoine Forqueray* (Bilthoven: A. B. Creyghton, 1973), pp. 14-7, also give only this tuning. In several of Clérambault's other cantatas, however, G_1 occurs with some frequency in parts labeled *viole* or *basse continue*. It seems unlikely that the instrument intended was the six-stringed viol tuned G_1, C, F, A, d, g that was described around the beginning of the seventeenth century by authors like Zacconi, Banchieri, Cerone, and Praetorius (Sibyl Marcuse, *Musical Instruments: A Comprehensive Dictionary* [New York: Doubleday & Company, Inc., 1964], p. 569). The only probable explanation appears to be that the lowest string was tuned down a step for such movements—*scordatura* was certainly not unusual at the time.

25. The music master in Molière's *Bourgeois Gentilhomme* counsels M. Jourdain in Act II, Scene 1, that in order to present weekly concerts he should hire three singers "qui seront accompagnées d'une basse de viole, d'un théorbe et d'un clavecin pour les basses continues, avec deux dessus de violon pour jouer les ritournelles." Quoted in Eppelsheim, *Das Orchester*, p. 151.

26. Michel Corrette, *Méthode théorique et pratique pour apprendre en peu de tems le violoncelle dans sa perfection* (Paris, 1741), Preface, p. A. Eppelsheim, *Das Orchester*, p. 41 and pp. 49-50, quotes from this passage and discusses it.

27. Sébastien de Brossard, *Dictionnaire de musique* (Paris, 1703), article "Violone." Eppelsheim, *Das Orchester*, p. 62, n. 72, also quotes the passage.

28. The full quotation is as follows: "Mrs. Montéclair, et Sagioni sont ceux qui ont joué les premiers de la contrebasse à l'Opéra de Paris, tous deux bons compositeurs: du temps de Mr de Lulli cet instrument étoit inconnu, ce n'est que bien du tems après luy qu'on a vû paroître la contre-basse à l'Opéra[;] encore ne servoit elle que dans les tempestes, dans les bruits souterrains et dans les invocations; et gardoit le tacet assez mal à propos dans les reste [*sic*]." Eppelsheim, *Das Orchester*, pp. 61-3, quotes this passage from Corrette's *Méthodes pour apprendre à joüer de la contre-basse à 3, à 4 et à 5 cordes, de la quinte ou alto et de la viole d'Orphée* (1781) and discusses three early tempest scenes in French operas, those in Marin Marais' *Alcione*, 1706; in Mathos' *Arion*, 1714; and in early-eighteenth-century revivals of Colasse's *Thétis et Pélée* (1689).

29. The instrumentation appearing in *privilèges* for 1712-13 and 1719, quoted in Eppelsheim, *Das Orchester*, p. 150.

30. "Quoy que la plus part des Autheurs de Sonates et de Cantates du commencement de ce Siècle, ayent composé les basses pour les Violes . . . cela n'empêche cependant pas que le Violoncelle ne les joüe avec applaudissement; ce qui ne sert pas peu à diminuer le succès de la Viole. . . ." Corrette, *Méthode théorique . . . pour . . . le violoncelle*, Preface, p. A.

31. These are by and large points appearing in one or more treatises of the time, such as J[acques] Boyvin, *Traté abrégé de l'accompagnement pour l'orgue et pour le clavecin* . . ., 2nd ed. (Paris, 1705); [Thomas] Campion, *Traité d'accompagnement et de composition, selon la règle des octaves de musique* . . . (Paris, 1716); Michel Corrette, *Le Maître de clavecin pour l'accompagnement, méthode théorique et pratique* (Paris, 1753) and *Prototipes, contenant des leçons d'accompagnement par demandes et par réponces* . . . (Paris, n. d.); D. Delair, *Traité de l'accompagnement pour le théorbe, et le clavessin* . . . (Paris, 1690); Georg Muffat, *An Essay on Thoroughbass* (1699), ed. Hellmut Federhofer ([Rome]: American Institute of Musicology, 1961); Jean-Philippe

Rameau, *Dissertation sur les différentes méthodes d'accompagnement pour le clavecin, ou pour l'orgue* (Paris, 1732) and *Code de musique pratique* . . . (Paris, 1760); and Michel de Saint-Lambert, *Les Principes du clavecin* . . . (Paris, 1702) and *Nouveau Traité de l'accompagnement du clavecin, de l'orgue, et des autres instruments* (Paris, 1707). Naturally, no two treatises are in complete accord on everything.

32. See quotation from Saint-Lambert in Eugène Borrel, *L'Interprétation de la musique française de Lully à la Révolution* (Paris: Alcan, 1934), p. 132.

33. Borrel, *L'Interprétation de la musique,* p. 118.

34. Delair, *Traité de l'accompagnement,* p. [2].

35. Rameau, *Dissertation,* p. 34, and *Code . . . pratique,* p. 74; Borrel, *L'Interprétation de la musique,* p. 118.

36. "Quand on accompagne un long récit, il est beau de demeurer quelquefois longtemps sur un accord quand la basse peut le permettre, et de ne donner les accords que par longs intervalles, supposé que la basse ne fasse que de longues notes. D'autres fois, après avoir frappé un accord rempli sur lequel on s'arrête longtemps, on rebat quelque note toute seule par cy par là, mais avec tant de ménagement qu'il semble que le Clavecin les rende de lui-même sans le consentement de l'Accompagnateur."

"D'autres fois, doublant les parties, on rebat toutes les notes l'une après l'autre d'une répétition continuelle, faisant faire au Clavecin un pétillement à peu près semblable à de la mousequeterie qui tire (trémolo [author's note]), mais après avoir fait cet agréable charivari pendant trois ou quatre mesures, on s'arrête tout court sur quelque grand accord harmonique (consonant), comme pour s'y reposer de la peine qu'on a eue à faire tout ce bruit." Quoted in Borrel, *L'Interprétation de la musique,* pp. 194-5. F. T. Arnold, in *The Art of Accompaniment from a Thorough-Bass as Practised in the XVIIth and XVIIIth Centuries* (1931; reprint: New York: Dover Publications, Inc., 1965), I:201, also quotes from this passage. In this section of his impressive study (I:172-202), Arnold summarizes Saint-Lambert's treatise of 1707. It is, however, the only French source to be included in 300 pages of such summaries.

37. Corrette, *Le Maître de clavecin* and *Prototipes, passim.*

38. Arnold, *The Art of Accompaniment,* I:373-5.

39. Paris, Bibliothèque de Sainte-Geneviève, MS No. 2374, bound together with a partial copy of it and other material by the Abbé A.-G. Pingré. I am indebted to Professor Albert Cohen for bringing this treatise to my attention.

40. ". . . Sur le second tems de la cadence [finale] on fait l'acord parfait majeur dans lequel on augmente la 7ᵉᵐᵉ mineure." Clérambault, "Règles," fol. 6 recto.

41. See Arnold, *The Art of Accompaniment,* II:803-35 and 861-2, and Borrel, *L'Interprétation de la musique,* pp. 107-13.

42. The meaning of all these symbols except x5 is given in Clérambault, "Règles," fol. 5 recto.

43. "M. Clérambault avoüe qu'il a conçû cette Règle à l'instant qu'on la lui montra. Je l'ay enseigné pareillement du premier coup d'oeil à plusieurs Maistres de mes amis, qui ont abandonné leurs anciens principes pour ne se servir que de ceux-ci." Campion, *Traité d'accompagnement,* p. 7. Clérambault's formal endorsement of Campion's method was published later, in the latter's *Addition au Traité d'accompagnement et de composition* . . . (Paris, 1730), p. 55:

"Approbation de Messieurs Clérambault
& Forqueray, Organistes.

"Nous avons lû avec plaisir cette addition au traité d'Accompagnement & de Composition du Sieur Campion, que nous avons jugé très conforme à la bonne harmonie, & par conséquent, très utile à tous ceux qui veulent accompagner de quelqu'instrument que ce soit, n'y ayant aucune Méthode aussi sensible, ni si abrégée que la Régle de l'Octave, dont nous nous servons nous-même préférablement dans nos Leçons, & dans nos chiffres. Fait à Paris ce vingtiéme Juillet 1729."

"M. FORQUERAY, CLÉRAMBAULT."

44. "Voyés les belles cantates de Mʳ Clérembault. Ces dissonances n'étoient pas apparament du goût de Mʳ Lully car on n'en trouve point dans ses Opéra." Corrette, *Le Maître de clavecin,* p. 52.

45. For two divergent views on the subject see Frederick Neumann, "The French *Inégales,* Quantz, and Bach," *Journal of the American Musicological Society* XVIII (Fall 1965):313-58; and Robert Donington, *The Interpretation of Early Music,* new vers. (New York: St. Martin's Press, 1974), pp. 452-63 and 665-70.

46. See Frederick Neumann, "External Evidence and Uneven Notes," *Musical Quarterly* LII (October 1966): 463-4.

47. Etienne Loulié, *Elements or Principles of Music* (1696), trans. and ed. Albert Cohen, *Musical Theorists in Translation* (Brooklyn, N. Y.: Institute of Medieval Music, [1965]), VI:30.

48. See Foster, "Louis-Nicolas Clérambault and His *Cantates françaises,*" I:236-9.

49. Eugène Borrel, "L'Interprétation de l'ancien récitatif français," *Revue de musicologie* XV (1931): 13-21.

50. Putnam Aldrich, "The Principal Agréments of the Seventeenth and Eighteenth Centuries: A Study in Musical Ornamentation" (Ph.D. diss., Harvard University, 1942); and "On the Interpretation of Bach's Trills," *Musical Quarterly* XLIX (July 1963): 289-310. Important additions found in Frederick Neumann, "Misconceptions about the French Trill in the 17th and 18th Centuries," *Musical Quarterly* L (April 1964): 188-206; "Notes on 'Melodic' and 'Harmonic' Ornaments," *Music Review* XXIX (November 1968): 249-56; and "Couperin and the Downbeat Doctrine for Appoggiaturas," *Acta Musicologica* XLI (January-June 1969): 71-85. These are the chief sources used in the following discussion.

51. For a more detailed treatment of Clérambault's ornaments see Foster, "Louis-Nicolas Clérambault and His *Cantates françaises,*" I:209-21.

52. Discussed by Neumann, "Misconceptions about the French Trill," pp. 199-203.

53. See especially Neumann, "Couperin and the Downbeat Doctrine."

54. Jean Rousseau, *Méthode claire, certaine et facile pour aprendre à chanter la musique,* 4th ed. (Paris, [1691]), p. 64.

Texts and Translations

L'Ile de Délos

[No. 1]

Agréable séjour qui dans le sein de l'onde
Par mille objets divers enchantez les regards,
Asile du repos, le Père des beaux arts
Vous préfère au reste du monde,
Il se fait un bonheur sur vos bords écartés
Des plaisirs innocents que vous lui présentez.

[No. 2]

Pour lui les filles de mémoire
De leurs divins accords font retentir les airs:
   Le protecteur de leur gloire
   Est l'objet de leurs concerts.

[No. 3]

   Paix tranquille,
   Dans cet asile
   Formez toujours
   Les plus aimables jours:

   Qu'une image
   Du premier âge
   Par mille plaisirs
   Comble nos innocents désirs.

[No. 4]

Terpsichore, au son des musettes,
Ranime des bergers les danses et les chants;
Et dans ces paisibles retraites
Annonce par ces mots le retour du printemps[:]

[No. 5]

   Régnez, brillante Flore,
   Embellissez ces bords,
   Faites partout éclore
   Vos plus riches trésors.

   Emaillez votre empire
   De nouvelles couleurs,
   Que l'aimable Zéphire
   Se couronne de fleurs.

   Régnez, etc.

L'Ile de Délos

(O pleasant abode, who amidst the waves
By a thousand different objects charm the gaze,
Restful haven, the Father of the arts
Prefers you to the rest of the world,
He finds happiness on your secluded shores
In the innocent pleasures that you offer him.)

(For him the Daughters of Memory
With their celestial harmonies make the air resound:
   The protector of their glory
   Is the object of their song.)

(O tranquil peace,
In this haven
Forever form
The loveliest of days:

So that an image
Of the first age
With a thousand pleasures
Might crown our innocent desires.)

(Terpsichore, to the sound of the bagpipes,
Revives the shepherds' dances and songs;
And, in this peaceful refuge,
Announces in these words the return of spring:)

(Reign, brilliant Flora,
Adorn these shores,
Let your richest treasures
Bloom in every part.

Bedeck your empire
With new colors,
So that gentle Zephyr
Might be crowned with flowers.

Reign, etc.)

[No. 6]

De ces champs fortunés la tristesse est bannie,
La Raison s'y repose au sein d'un doux loisir;
   La Déesse de l'harmonie
Y sait unir toujours la Sagesse au plaisir;
   Sur ce rivage solitaire
D'un accord si charmant naissent les jours heureux,
    La Sagesse jamais n'a rien de trop sévère,
    Et jamais le plaisir n'a rien de dangereux.

(From these happy fields sorrow is banished,
Reason reposes there amidst sweet idleness;
   There the Goddess of harmony
Is ever able to combine Wisdom with pleasure;
   On these solitary shores
Blissful days arise from such charming accord,
    Wisdom is never too austere,
    And pleasure never dangerous.)

[No. 7]

Coulez dans une paix profonde,
Coulez, moments délicieux,
Imitez le cours de l'onde
Qui vient arroser ces lieux.

Le long d'un si charmant rivage
Elle coule parmi les fleurs,
C'est une fidèle image
De nos tranquilles douceurs.

Coulez, etc.

(Flow in profound peace,
Flow, sweet moments,
Imitate the coursing of the stream
That comes to water these regions.

Passing by this charming strand
It flows amongst the flowers,
It is a faithful image
Of our peaceful diversions.

Flow, etc.)

[No. 8]

Nos désirs sont comblés, sous ce naissant ombrage
Je vois des doctes soeurs l'arbitre souverain,

(Our desires are crowned, in this burgeoning arbor
I see the sovereign arbiter of the learned sisters;)

[No. 9]

Tout s'empresse à lui rendre hommage,
Les arbres réjouis agitent leur feuillage,
L'air est plus pur et plus serein,
Les oiseaux à l'envi redoublent leur ramage;
   Ecoutez les sons touchants
   De la tendre Philomèle,
   L'Echo s'éveille à ses chants
   Et les redit après elle.

(All hasten to render him homage,
The gladdened trees shake their foliage,
The air is more pure and serene,
The birds, vying with each other, redouble their song;
   Hear the touching sounds
   Of the tender Philomela,
   Echo awakens to her song
   And repeats it after her.)

[No. 10]

Durez toujours, tranquilles jeux,
Prenez la Sagesse pour guide,
Dans ce séjour heureux
C'est elle qui préside.

Lorsque vous marchez sur ses pas,
Quel spectacle est plus agréable[?]
Elle vous prête des appas,
Et vous la rendez plus aimable.

Durez toujours, etc.

(Live forever, gentle pastimes,
Take Wisdom as your guide,
In this happy abode
It is she who presides.

When you follow in her steps,
What sight is more agreeable?
She lends you charm,
And you make her lovelier.

Live forever, etc.)

La Muse de l'Opéra

[No. 1]

[No. 2]

Mortels, pour contenter vos désirs curieux
Cessez de parcourir tous les climats du monde,
Par le puissant effort de l'art qui nous seconde,
Ici tout l'univers se découvre à vos yeux.

[No. 3]

Au son des trompettes bruyantes
Mars vient embellir ce séjour,
Diane, avec toute sa cour,
Vous offre des fêtes galantes,
Et mille chansons éclatantes
Réveillent l'Echo d'alentour.

Des bergers, la troupe légère,
Vient folâtrer sur ces gazons,
A leurs danses, à leurs chansons
On voit que le Dieu de Cythère
Leur a donné de ses leçons.

Au son, etc.

[No. 4]

Mais quel bruit interrompt
Ces doux amusements?
Le soleil s'obscurcit,
La mer s'enfle et s'irrite,
Dieux! quels terribles flots!
Et quels mugissements!
La terre tremble, l'air s'agite,
Tous les vents déchaînés,
Mille effrayants éclairs
Semblent confondre l'univers.
Quels sifflements affreux!
Quel horrible tonnerre!
Le ciel est-il jaloux
Du repos de la terre?

[No. 5]

Non, les dieux, attendris par nos cris éclatants,
Ramènent les beaux jours de l'aimable printemps.

[No. 6]

Oiseaux, qui sous ces feuillages
Formez des accents si doux,
L'Amour, quand il vous engage,
Vous traite bien mieux que nous;
Il n'est jamais parmi vous
Jaloux, trompeur, ni volage.

La Muse de l'Opéra

Prelude

(Mortals, to satisfy your curious desires
Cease to wander through every earthly clime,
With the mighty efforts of art to assist us,
Here the whole universe is revealed to your eyes.)

(To the sound of the noisy trumpets
Mars comes to adorn these regions,
Diana, with all her court,
Offers you elegant festivities,
And a thousand ringing songs
Awaken the surrounding Echo.

Some shepherds, the gentle band,
Come to frolic on the green,
Their dances, their songs
Show that the god of Cythera
Has given them lessons.

To the sound, etc.)

(But what noise interrupts
These gentle amusements?
The sun grows dark,
The sea billows and storms,
O gods! what dreadful waves!
And what roaring!
The earth trembles, the air seethes,
All the winds unleashed,
A thousand terrifying thunderbolts
Seem to confound the universe.
What fearful whistling!
What horrible thunder!
Are the heavens jealous
Of earth's repose?)

(No, the gods, moved by our piercing cries,
Restore the fair days of lovely spring.)

(Birds, who in this leafy bower
Form your accents so sweet:
When Love entangles you,
You are treated far better than we;
With you he is never
Jealous, deceitful, nor fickle.)

[No. 7]

Vos concerts, heureux oiseaux,
Eveillent trop tôt l'aurore,
Laissez les mortels encore
Plongés au sein du repos.

(Your singing, happy birds,
Awakens too soon the dawn,
Let mortals be—still
Plunged in the depths of repose.)

[No. 8]

Mais quels nouveaux accords dont l'horreur est
	extrême?
Qui fait ouvrir le séjour infernal?
Que de démons sortis de ce gouffre
	fatal!
Les implacables soeurs suivent Pluton lui-même.

(But what are these new chords, so filled with
	horror?
Who has unsealed the infernal region?
What a host of demons has sprung from that fateful
	abyss!
The unappeasable sisters are in pursuit of Pluto
	himself.)

[No. 9]

Ne craignons rien, un changement heureux
Vient nous offrir de doux présages;
Et les démons, changés sous d'aimables images,
Amusent nos regards par d'agréables jeux.

(We have nothing to fear, a happy change of events
Bodes well for us;
And the demons, transformed by pleasant disguise,
Entertain us with gay diversions.)

[No. 10]

Ce n'est qu'une belle chimère
Qui satisfait ici vos voeux;
Eh! n'êtes-vous pas trop heureux
Qu'on vous séduise pour vous plaire?

(It is nothing but a pretty illusion
That satisfies your wishes here;
Oh! aren't you happy
To be deceived only to be amused?

Dans ce qui flatte vos désirs
Croyez tout ce qu'on fait paraître;
On voit s'envoler les plaisirs
Lorsque l'on cherche à les connaître.

In that which flatters your desires
Believe all that is made to appear;
Pleasures vanish
When you try to understand them.

Ce n'est qu'une, etc.

It is nothing, etc.)

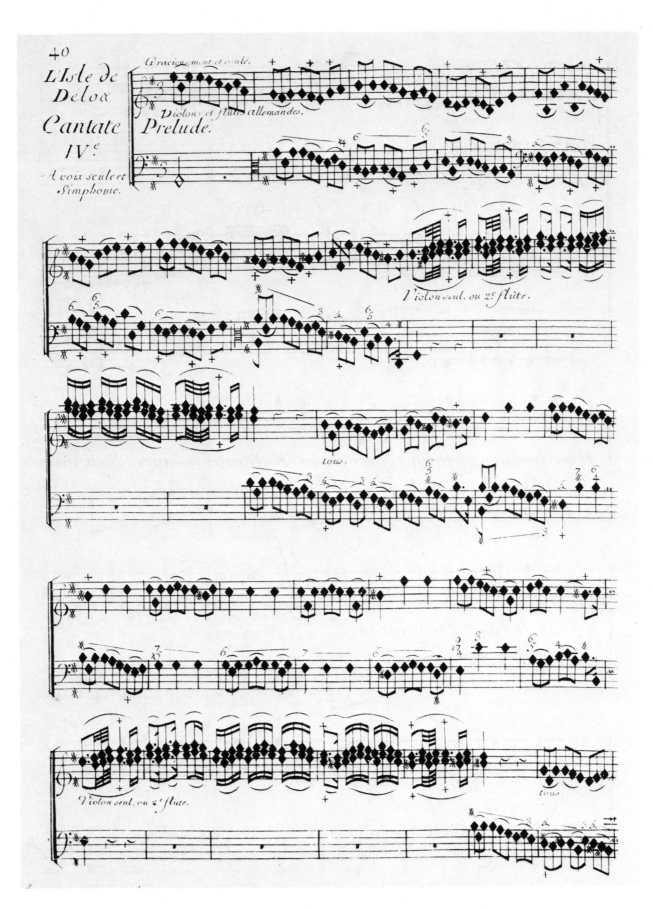

Plate I. First page of *L'Ile de Délos*, p. 40 in the third book of cantatas.
(Courtesy, University of Michigan Library)

Plate II. *La Muse de l'Opéra*, p. 16: conclusion of [No. 4], Tempête; [No. 5], Récitatif; beginning of [No. 6], Air. (Courtesy, University of Michigan Library)

L'ILE DE DELOS

L'Ile de Délos

Cantate à voix seule et symphonie

[No. 1] Prélude [et air]

Gracieusement et coulé

4

(a) Voice: Eighth-notes unequal throughout movement:

Par mille ob-jets di - vers en-chan - tez les re - gards,

A - si - le du re - pos,_____

_____ le Pè - re des beaux arts Vous pré - fère au res-

Viole
[seule]

-te du mon- de, Il se fait un bon-

-heur sur vos bords é - car - tés Des plai - sirs in - no-

-cents que vous lui pré-sen- tez.

[No. 2] Air (a)

Doucement

[Violons]

[Voix]

Pour lui les fil- les de mé- moi- re

[B.c. : Clavecin et Basse de Viole]

(a) Quarter-notes probably unequal throughout movement—approximately

(b) The harpsichordist should repeat the tied bass note once or twice—for example, on the first beats of mm. 3–4.

8

De leurs di-vins ac- cords   font re-ten-tir les airs:

airs: Le pro-tec- teur de leur gloi-   re

Est l'ob- jet   de leurs con- certs,   Le pro-tec-

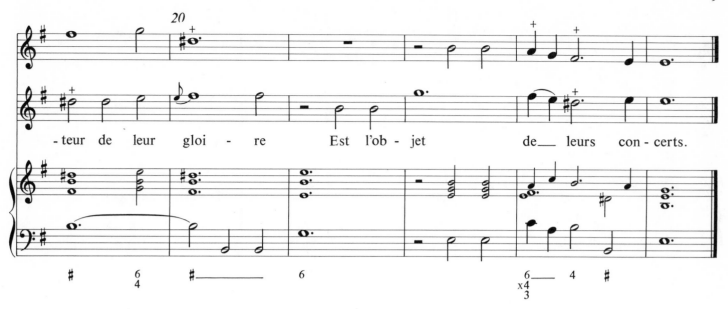

-teur de leur gloi - re   Est l'ob - jet   de__ leurs con - certs.

[No. 3] Air de Musette (a)

Doucement et gracieusement

[Violons]

[Voix]

[B.c.: Clavecin et Basse de Viole]

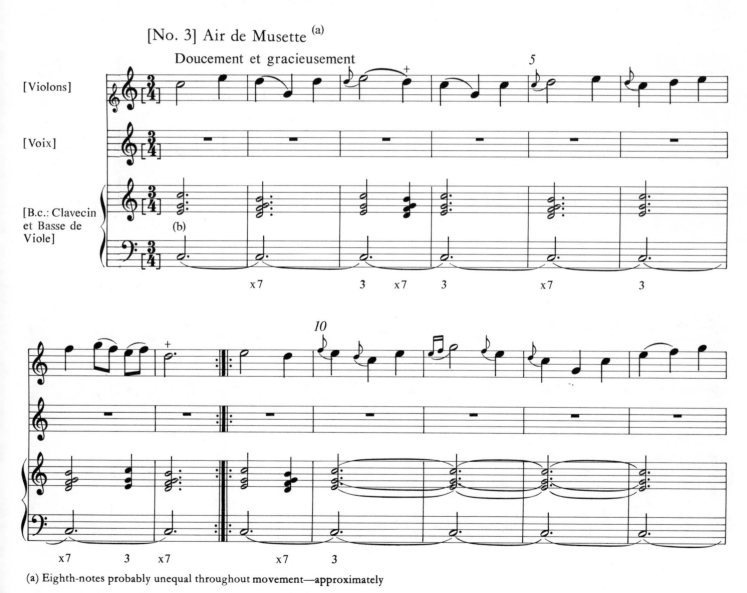

(a) Eighth-notes probably unequal throughout movement—approximately

(b) The harpsichordist should repeat the tied bass note (and chord, where tied) on the first beats of some measures.

[Fine]

doux

Paix tran - quil - le, Dans

cet a - si - le For - mez tou - jours Les plus ai - ma - bles__ jours: Qu'une i -

On reprend l'Air de musette
à la page précédente
[D.C. al Fine]

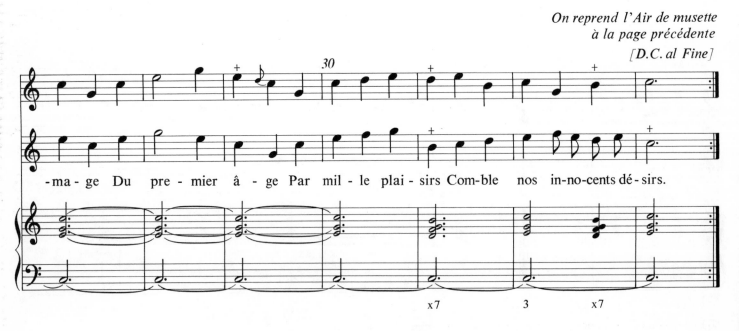

-ma - ge Du pre - mier â - ge Par mil - le plai - sirs Com - ble nos in - no - cents dé - sirs.

[No. 4 Récitatif mesuré](a)

Violons

[Voix]

(b) Terp-si-chore, au son des__ mu - set-tes, Ra - ni - me des ber-

[B.c.: Clavecin et Basse de Viole]

-gers les dan - ses__ et les chants; Et dans ces pai-si-bles re - trai - tes An-

Récitatif

[No. 5] Air gai (c)

Reprise

-non - ce par ces mots le re - tour du prin - temps[:]

(a) Eighth-notes probably unequal throughout movement—approximately

(b) The text of No. 4 is a quotation from Clérambault's cantata *La Musette,* from the second book of cantatas, 1713.

(c) Unless the tempo taken is too fast to lend itself to inequality in this movement, eighth-notes should probably be as in (a) above.

12

Reg - nez,_____

_____ bril - lan - te____ Flo ____ re, Em - bel - lis-sez____ ces bords,

Fai - tes par-tout é - clo ____ re Vos plus ri ____ ches tré - sors.

doux

fort

nez,_____ bril -lan - te__ Flo - re, Em - bel -lis -sez__ ces

bords, Fai-tes par-tout é - clo - re Vos plus ri - ches tré - sors,

Fai-tes par-tout é - clo - re Vos plus ri - ches tré - sors.

E-mail-lez votre em - pi – re De nou-vel - les cou-leurs,

E-mail-lez votre em - pi – re De nou-vel – les cou-leurs, Que l'ai-

-ma - ble___ Zé - phi - re Se cou-ron-

- ne de fleurs, Que l'ai - ma - ble Zé - phi - re Se cou-

- ron - - - - ne de fleurs.

[No. 6] Récitatif

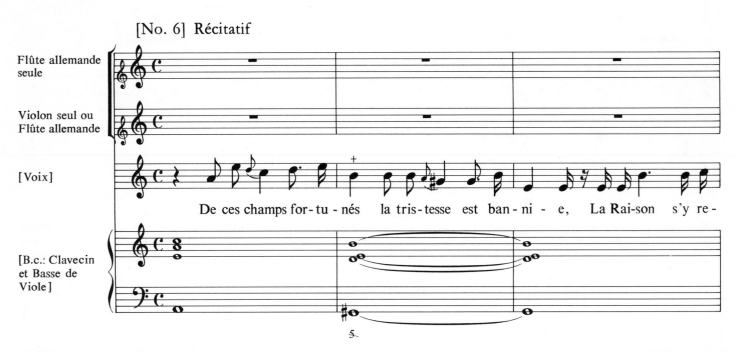

Flûte allemande
seule

Violon seul ou
Flûte allemande

[Voix]

[B.c.: Clavecin
et Basse de
Viole]

De ces champs for-tu-nés la tris-tesse est ban-ni-e, La Rai-son s'y re-

-pose au sein d'un doux loi-sir; La Dé-es-se de l'har-mo-ni-e Y sait u-nir tou-

19

[No. 7] Air tendre

Lentement et coulé

21

-ments dé-li-ci-eux,   I-mi-tez   le__cours de l'on - de Qui vient____ ar-ro-

2ᵉ Flûte allemande
ou Violon *seul*

- ser____   ces lieux.

Cou-

-lez,_____ mo - ments dé - li - ci - eux, I - mi - tez le__ cours de

l'on - de Qui vient____ ar - ro - ser____ ces lieux.

2ᵉ Flûte allemande
ou Violon *seul*

Le long   d'un si char-mant ri -

2ᵉ Flûte allemande
ou Violon *seul*

-va - ge El-le cou -   le par - mi les fleurs,

C'est u - ne fi-dèle i - ma - ge De nos tran - quil-

x4   6   6   6

- les dou - ceurs,   C'est u -ne fi-dèle i - ma - ge De nos tran -

5 3 7 #   6 x4 6 6   #
      4   4

- quil - - - les____ dou-ceurs.   Cou-

[No. 8] Récitatif

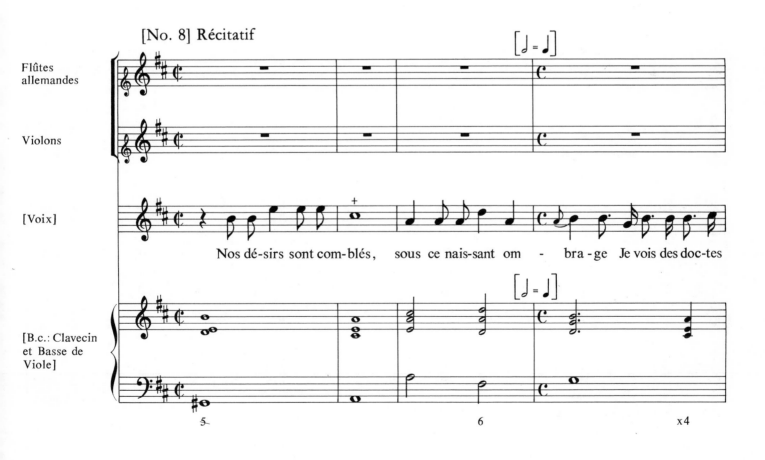

Flûtes
allemandes

Violons

[Voix]

Nos dé-sirs sont com-blés, sous ce nais-sant om — bra-ge Je vois des doc-tes

[B.c.: Clavecin
et Basse de
Viole]

[No. 9 Récitatif mesuré]

Gracieusement et coulé

soeurs l'ar-bi-tre sou-ve - rain,

Tout s'em-

[Viole tacet]

-presse à lui rendre hom-ma - ge,

Les ar - bres ré-jou-

-is a - gi-tent leur feuil - la - ge,

L'air est plus pur et plus se - rein,

[1ᵉ Flûte allemande]

2ᵉ Flûte allemande *ou* Violon *seul*

Les oi - seaux   à l'en - vi re-dou-blent leur ra - ma - ge;

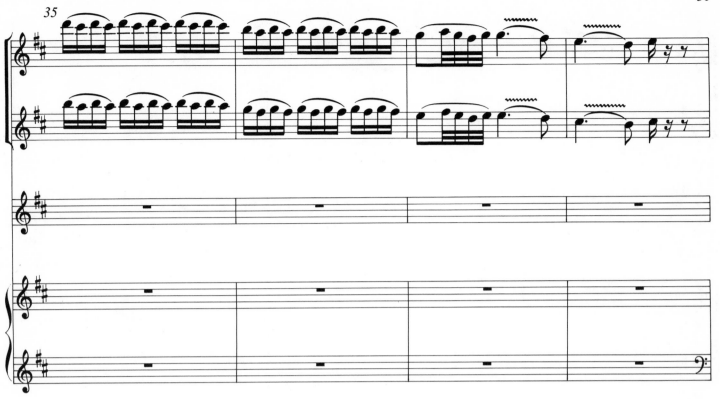

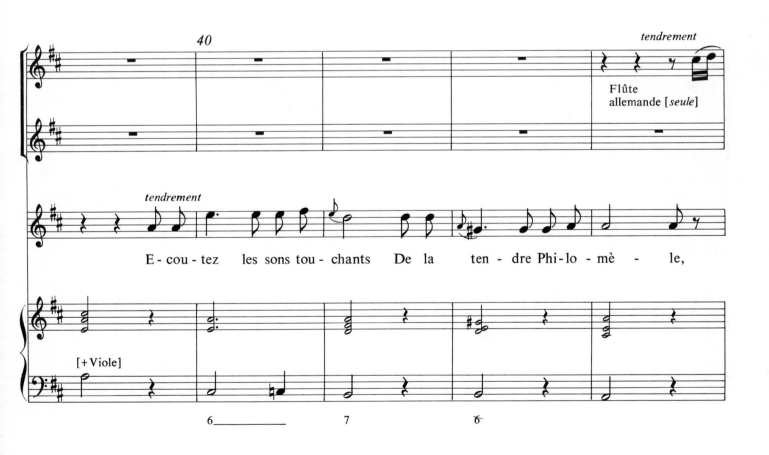

E - cou - tez les sons tou - chants De la ten - dre Phi-lo - mè - le,

[+Viole]

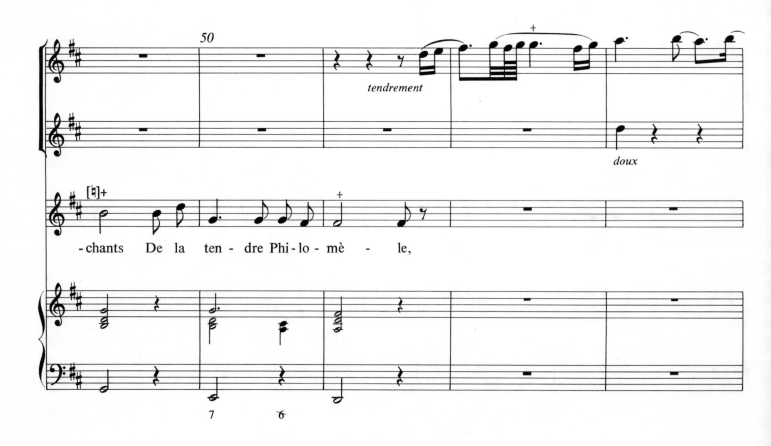

L'E-cho s'é - veille à ses chants Et les re -

-dit a - près el - le.

écho   fort   écho

plus doux

légèrement

L'E-cho s'é-veille à   ses

fort

tendrement

[fort]   écho

doux

chants   Et les re - dit   a - près el   -   le.

6   6   5   6   6   4   3
                  5

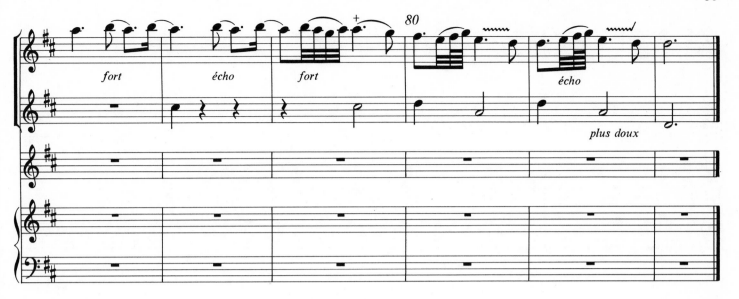

[No. 10] Air ^(a)

Doucement sans lenteur

Violons

[Voix]

[B.c.: Clavecin et Basse de Viole]

(a) Throughout the movement, ♩♩ and ♩·♪ = ♪ ³♪ (♪ ♪ = ♪ ³♪), ♩· ♪ = ♩ ³♪, except in the figure ♪♪ ♪·♪·♪·♪, which should be unaltered.

38

LA MUSE DE L'OPERA

La Muse de l'Opéra

Cantate à voix seule et symphonie

(a) Eighth-notes probably unequal throughout movement – approximately

[No. 2]   Récitatif

Trompette et premier dessus de Violon [et de Hautbois]

Deuxième dessus de Violon [et de Hautbois]

[Voix]

Mor-tels, pour con-ten - ter   vos dé-sirs   cu - ri - eux   Ces -

Timbales et Basses de Violon

[B.c.: Clavecin et Basse de Viole]

-sez   de par-cou-rir tous les cli-mats   du   mon - de,   Par   le   puis-sant   ef-

-fort   de l'art qui nous se - con-de,   I - ci   tout l'u-ni-vers   se dé-couvre à   vos

[No. 3] Air gai

yeux.

Basses de Viole et continues
[+ Bassons]

(a) Voice: Eighth-notes probably unequal throughout movement (except in mm. 69 – 74) – approximately

(b) "These double notes are placed here for the convenience of the singer."

Mars vient em-bel - lir ce sé - jour,

[+bsns.]

48

tou - te sa cour, Vous of - fre des fê - tes ga - lan -

- tes, Et mil - le chan - sons é - cla - tan - tes Ré - veil - lent l'E -

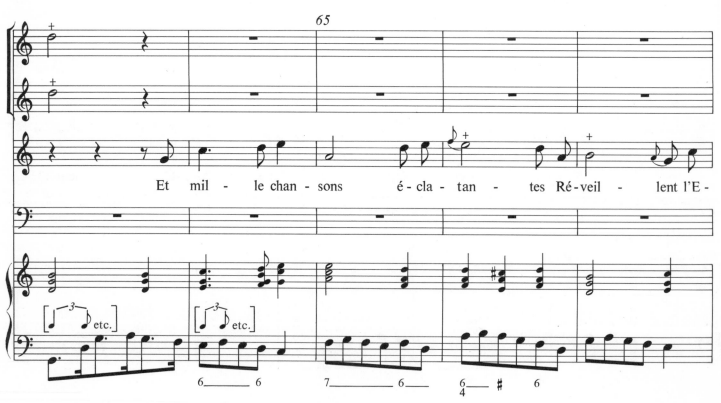

Des ber - gers,   la

54

(a) The harpsichordist should repeat the bass note on the first beat of some measures here and in mm. 123 –125, 138 – 141.

ces _____ ga - zons, A leurs dan - ses, à leurs chan-

-sons, On voit que le Dieu de Cy - thè - re Leur a don-

-né de __ ses __ le - çons,

130

doux
[+ vls.,
– htbs.]

A leurs dan - ses, à leurs chan - sons, On

voit que le Dieu de Cy - thè - re Leur a don -

135

Hautbois
[– vls.]

-né de ses___ le - çons.

[+] Bassons

Au son des trom - pet - tes bruy - an - tes

Mars vient em-bel - lir ce sé - jour,   Di - ane, a - vec

[No. 4] Tempête

Fort et marqué

Flûte allemande
seule

[Violons]

[Voix]

Basses
de Violon

Contrebasse et
B.c.:
[Clav. et Basse
de Viole]

[Clav.:   etc.]   x7

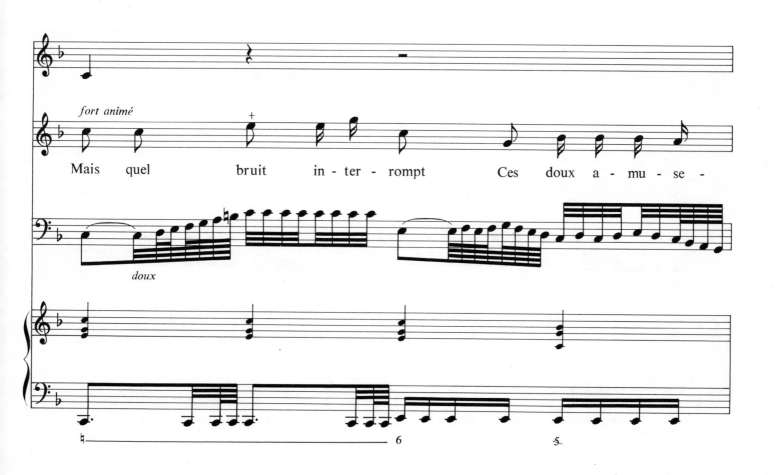

63

mer   s'enfle   et   s'ir - ri - te,

fort

fort

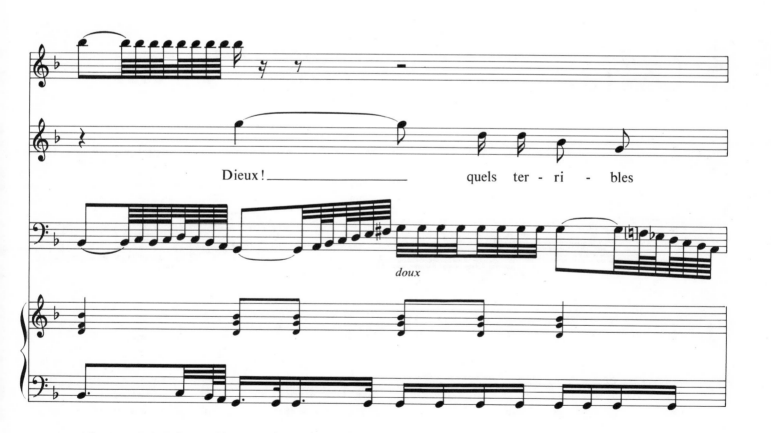

Dieux !_____   quels ter - ri - bles

doux

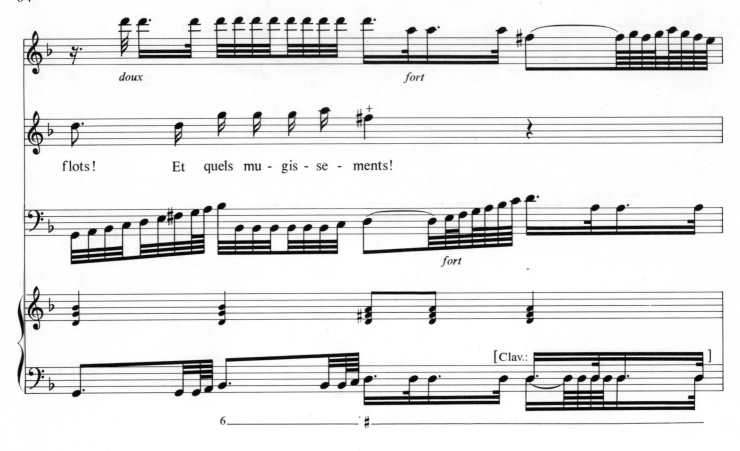

doux · fort

flots! Et quels mu - gis - se - ments!

fort

[Clav.:]

6 #

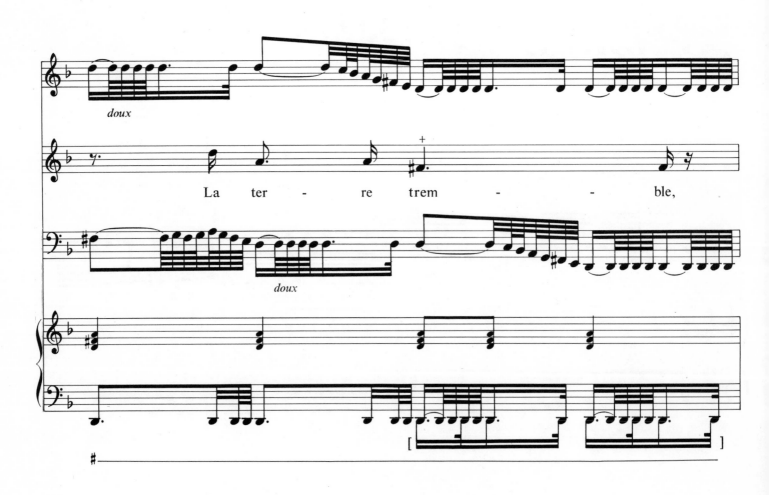

doux

La ter - re trem - - ble,

doux

#

l'air   s'a - gi - te,

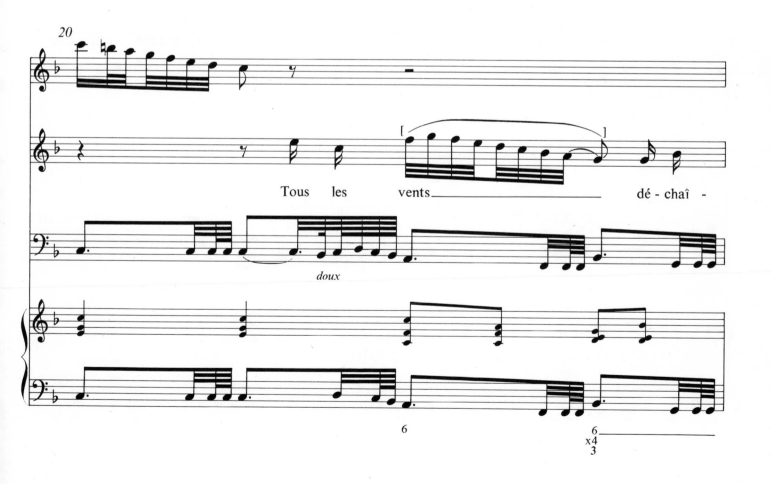

Tous   les   vents_____ dé - chaî -

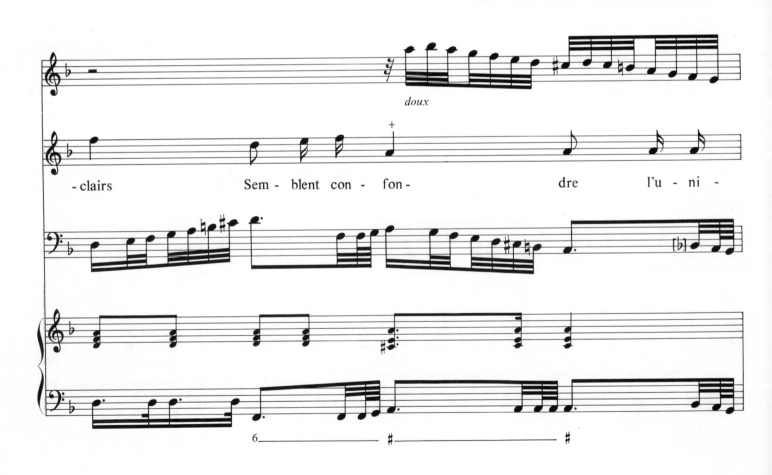

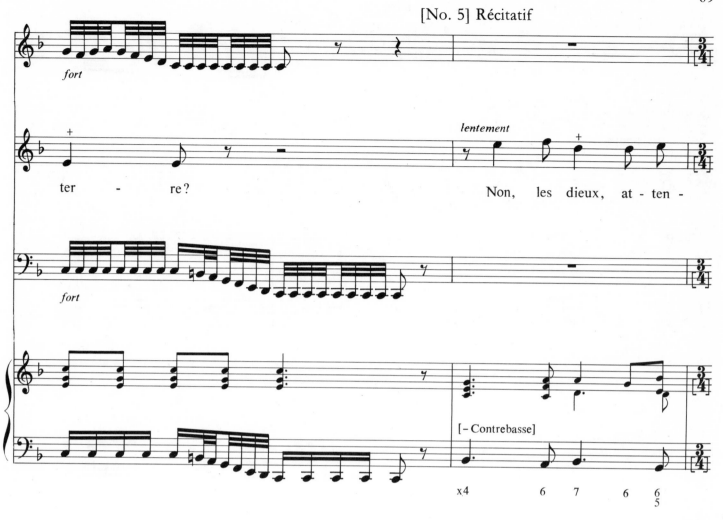

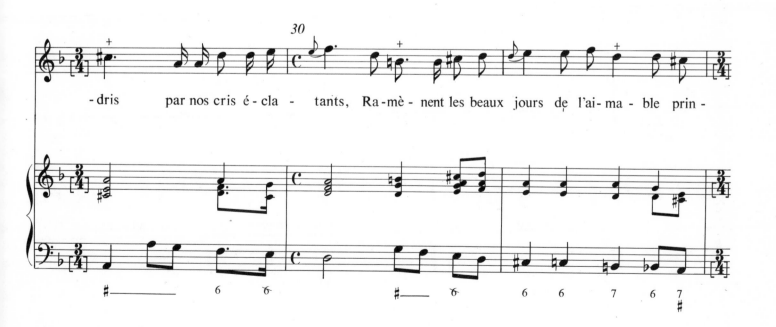

[No. 6] Air

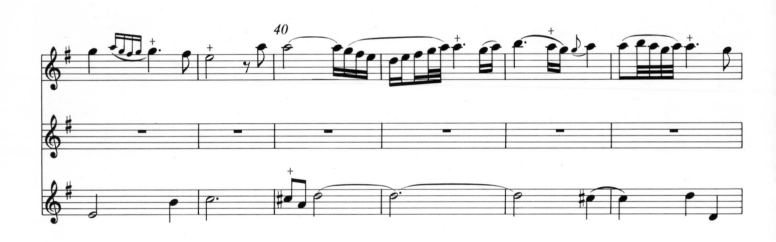

Oi - seaux, qui sous ces feuil - la - ges For - mez des ac - cents_____ si

vous Ja - loux, trom - peur, ni vo - la - - ge.

[No. 7]   Sommeil (a)

Tous.
Violons

[Voix]

[B.c.: Clavecin
et Basses de
Viole]

(a) Eighth-notes probably unequal throughout movement – approximately

Vos con - certs, heu-reux __ oi-seaux, E - veil-lent trop tôt l'au - ro - re, Lais - sez les mor-tels en - co - re Plon - gés au sein du re - pos,

[No. 8] Prélude infernal
Lentement, fort, et marqué

-co - re Plon - gés au sein du re - pos.

Mais _____ quels nou-veaux ac - cords dont l'hor -

[Récitatif]

Que de dé-mons sor - tis   de ce

très vite

gouf - fre fa - tal!

[Récitatif]

Les im - pla - ca - bles   soeurs   sui - vent Plu - ton lui - mê - me.

[No. 9] Récitatif

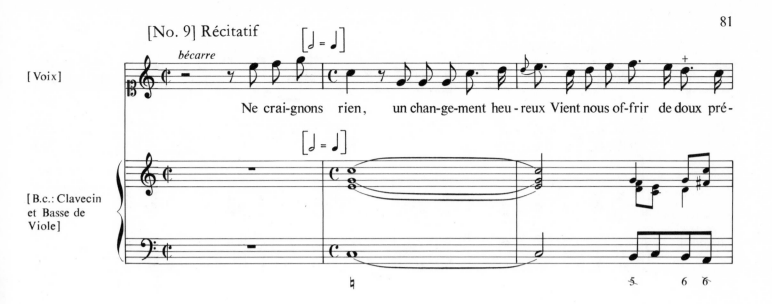

Ne crai-gnons rien, un chan-ge-ment heu-reux Vient nous of-frir de doux pré-

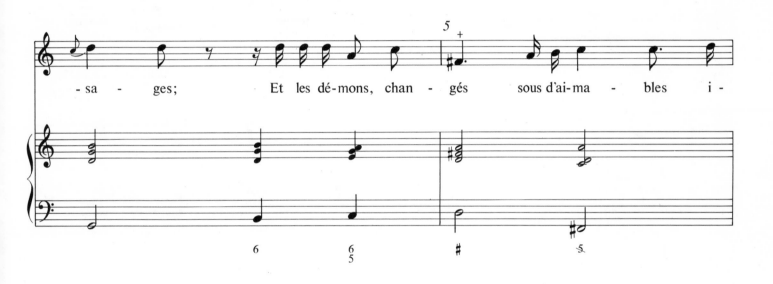

-sa - ges; Et les dé-mons, chan - gés sous d'ai-ma - bles i -

-ma - ges, A-mu - sent nos re - gards par d'a-gré-a - bles jeux.

[attacca]

[No. 10] Air

(a) *Piqué* in this movement probably refers to the performance of the dotted-eighth and sixteenth-note rhythms as written, rather than assimilated into triplet rhythm. See Preface.

Qui sa - tis - fait i - ci vos voeux;

Ce

n'est qu'u - ne bel - le chi - mè - re Qui sa - tis - fait i - ci vos

voeux; Eh! n'ê - tes - vous pas trop heu - reux Qu'on vous sé - dui - se pour vous

Dans ce qui flat - te vos dé - sirs Croy - ez tout ce qu'on fait pa -

- raî - tre: On voit s'en - vo - ler les plai -

- sirs Lors-que l'on cherche à les con - naî - tre,

Suggested interpretation of ornaments, mm. 104–107, 116–119.